A MODERN METHOD FOR VIOLA SCALES

Rob Thomas

To access audio visit:
www.halleonard.com/mylibrary

Enter Code
2073-4688-2163-9332

BERKLEE PRESS
Editor in Chief: Jonathan Feist
Senior Vice President Pre-College, Online, and Professional Programs/
CEO and Cofounder of Berklee Online: Debbie Cavalier

ISBN: 978-0-87639-208-9

Berklee Press

1140 Boylston Street
Boston, MA 02215-3693 USA
(617) 747-2146

Visit Berklee Press Online at
www.berkleepress.com

Berklee Online

Study music online at
online.berklee.edu

DISTRIBUTED BY
HAL•LEONARD®
7777 W. BLUEMOUND RD. P.O. BOX 13819
MILWAUKEE, WISCONSIN 53213

Visit Hal Leonard Online
www.halleonard.com

Berklee Press, a publishing activity of Berklee College of Music, is a not-for-profit educational publisher.
Available proceeds from the sales of our products are contributed to the scholarship funds of the college.

CONTENTS

PREFACE

Early in my development as a jazz player, I realized that my classical training—although invaluable in so many ways—was falling short. The jazz vocabulary that I was expected to transpose to all twelve keys (without benefit of notation) was at times proving difficult or impossible to execute. In a number of keys, my left hand was encountering a confusing smorgasbord of fingering options. And in general, some of my normal violinistic impulses seemed to produce unsatisfactory results as I began the serious study of jazz improvisation.

I was fortunate to play with some skilled musicians who showed me the way—who could get around on their instruments with great fluency in any key, and who had learned to phrase like the masters. The trouble was, none of them played the violin. So I began to organize my materials, and set about trying to level the playing field.

The method presented here grew organically out of the process of developing, reorganizing, and refining the aforementioned materials. It also resulted from ongoing efforts to share my experience with new generations of like-minded string players.

ABOUT THE AUDIO

To access the accompanying audio, go to www.halleonard.com/mylibrary and enter the code found on the first page of this book. This will grant you instant access to every example. Examples with accompanying audio are marked with an audio icon.

CHAPTER 1

Single-String Frames

The scale fingerings in this book can be played easily if you have a grasp of the following whole-step/half-step patterns. There are a total of eight possibilities when you place all four fingers on a string without using any extensions. In other words, if you are playing only half steps and/or whole steps, there are eight possible shapes, or "frames," you can play. The five shown below are the ones we'll use in the major-scale fingerings that follow.

The first frame is three consecutive whole steps, which we'll abbreviate as www.

FIG. 1.1. www Fingering Frame

Arbitrarily putting the first finger on E♭, in standard notation, the "www" frame looks like figure 1.2.

www: whole, whole, whole

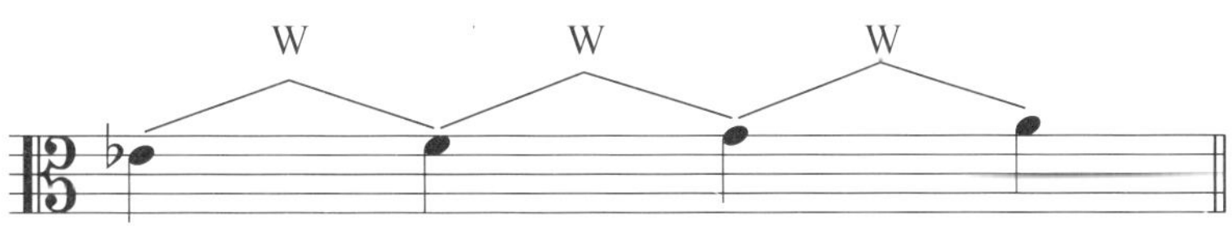

FIG. 1.2. www from E♭

You can play the frames from any first-finger position; the E♭ is just an example.

Here are the other frames. Note: Usually, the frame diagrams are presented vertically, to match how we see them on the fingerboard, but we'll present them horizontally in this chapter to make a clearer connection to the notation.

wwh: two whole steps and a half step

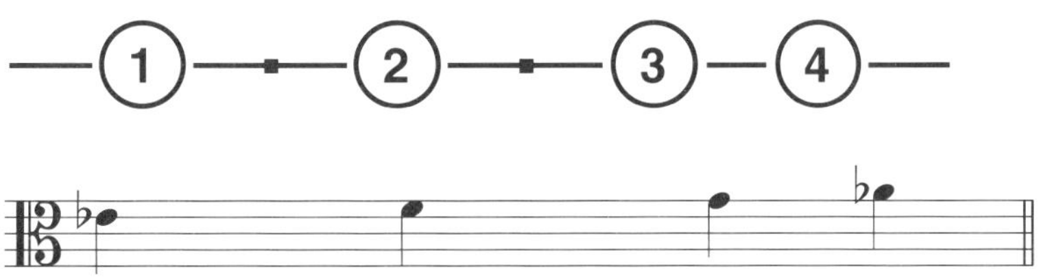

FIG. 1.3. wwh Fingering

whw: whole step, half step, whole step

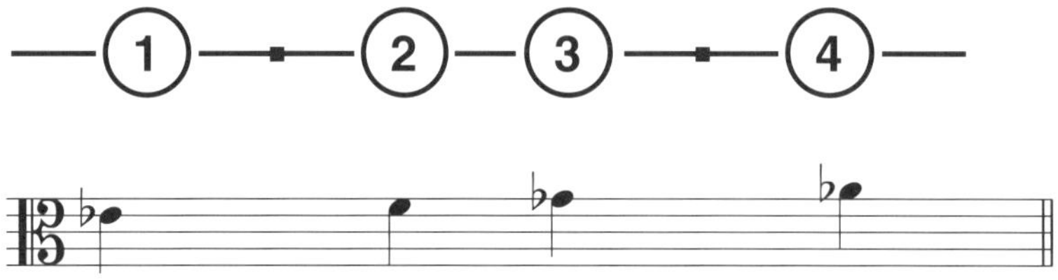

FIG. 1.4. whw Fingering

hww: half step, whole step, whole step

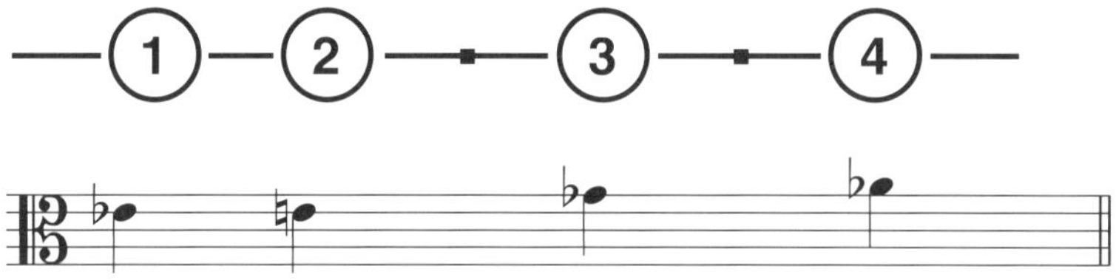

FIG. 1.5. hww Fingering

hwh: half step, whole step, half step

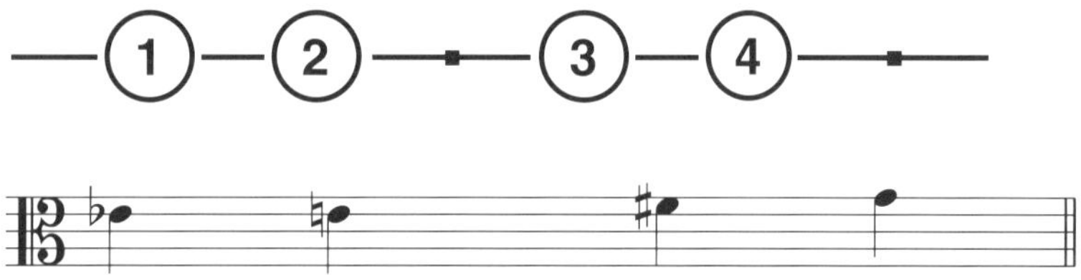

FIG. 1.6. hwh Fingering

Here are the other three patterns, not found in the major scales, but important just the same.

whh: whole step, half step, half step

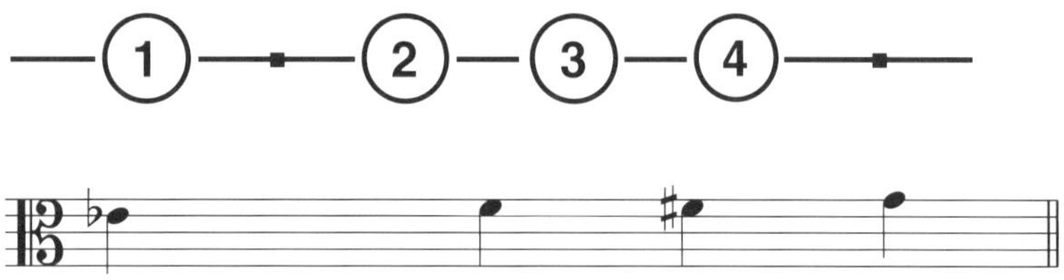

FIG. 1.7. whh Fingering

hhw: half step, half step, whole step

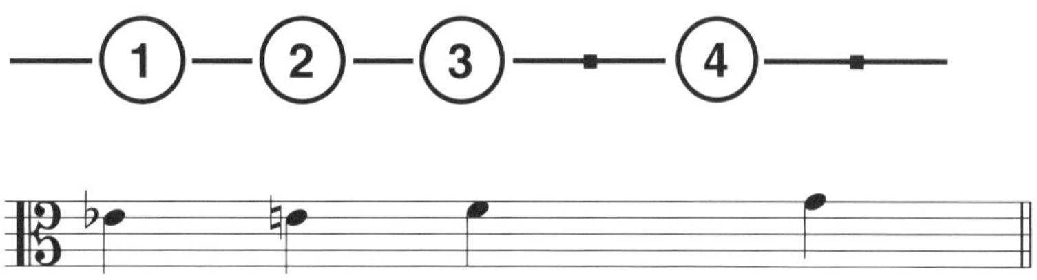

FIG. 1.8. hhw Fingering

hhh: half step, half step, half step

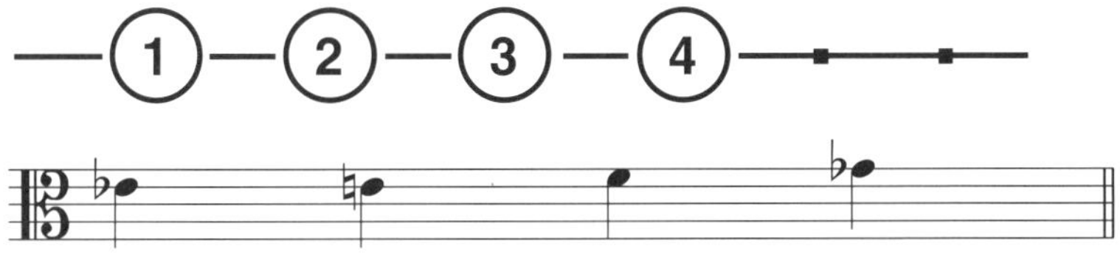

FIG. 1.9. hhh Fingering

Figure 1.10 presents the single-string frames again in a convenient reference, and in an ideal order for practice. You can play them from any first-finger placement on any string. Use this chart to practice them in isolation.

In addition to the five frames used for major scales, the three additional frames (grayed out) are presented (whh, hhw, hhh) that are used for some additional scales, such as the diminished scales, blues scales, and chromatic scales, but are outside the scope of this book. Frames 1, 2, 3, 5, and 6 are used in the major scale, and are thus the most relevant for now. Practice them all in the order shown in figure 1.10, to build facility and for future use.

1	www	
2	wwh	
3	whw	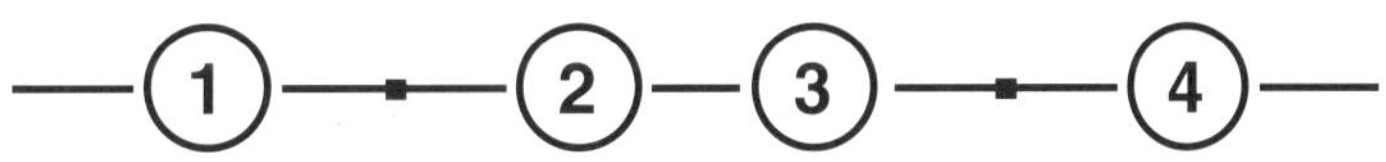
4	whh	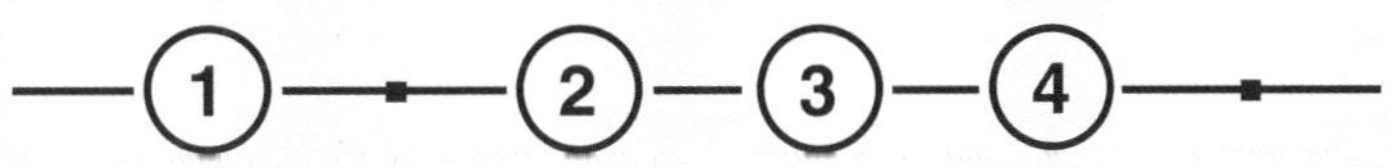
5	hww	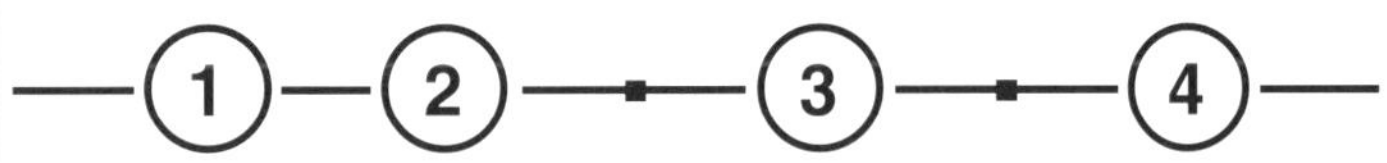
6	hwh	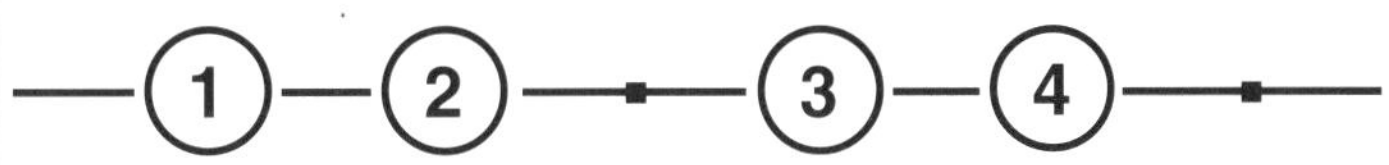
7	hhw	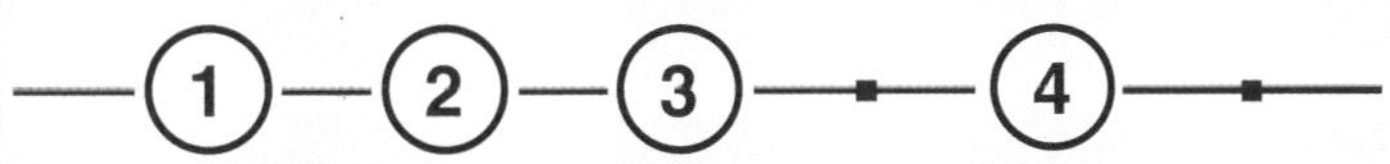
8	hhh	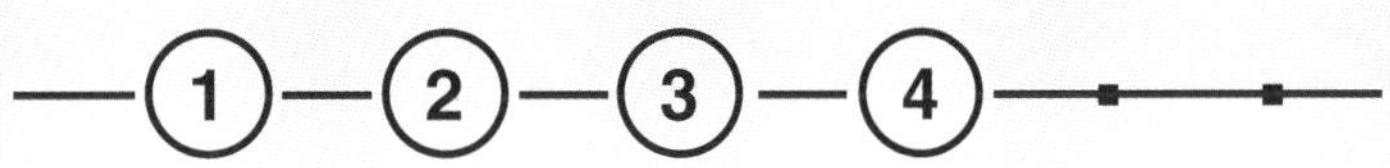

FIG. 1.10. Single-String Finger Frame Practice Chart

FRAME ETUDE

Practice the etude in figure 1.12, using it to develop facility with each of these single-string fingering frames. Repeat it using the note-group variations shown in figure 1.11. The fingering is 1-2-3-4 for each group of notes.

The etude is designed to be played from any first-finger placement. You can put your first finger on any note, any position, any string, and play the melodic patterns and note groups shown here starting from E♭/D♯.

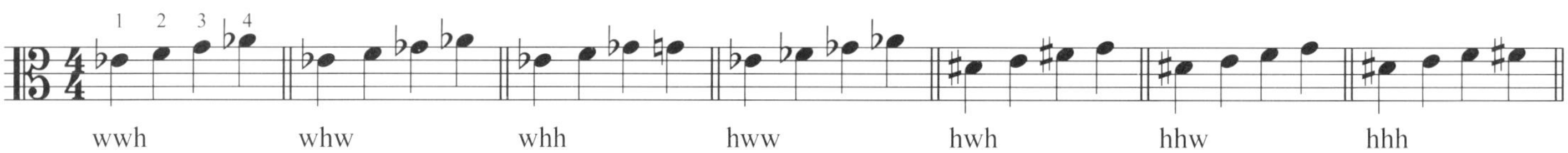

FIG. 1.11. Note-Group Variations

FIG. 1.12. Frame Etude

CHAPTER 2

Four-String Frames

A four-string frame is a combination of four single-string frames. Here's a four-string frame for the key of C major, diagrammed here as a bird's-eye view of the fingerboard. The vertical lines represent the C, G, D, and A strings, left to right.

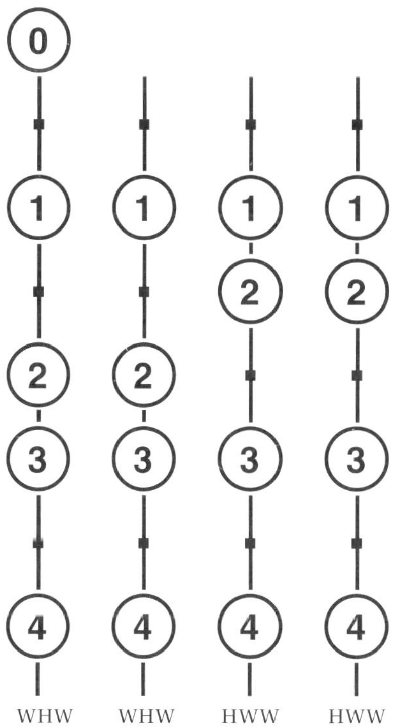

FIG. 2.1. C Major Four-String Frame

The four-string frame includes every note in the key of C that's available in first position. Here it is notated:

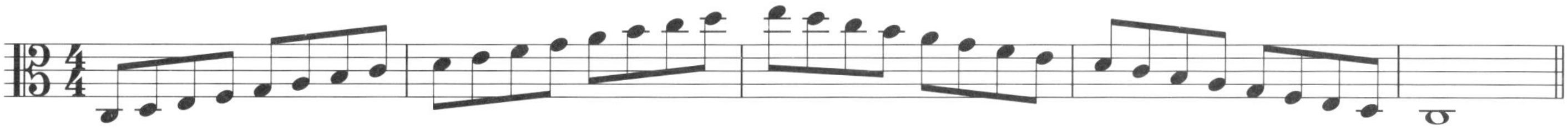

FIG. 2.2. C Major Scale Notation

There is a tendency among non-classical players to use open strings more frequently than classical players do. Let's look at the same notes with open strings replacing fourth finger G, D, and A.

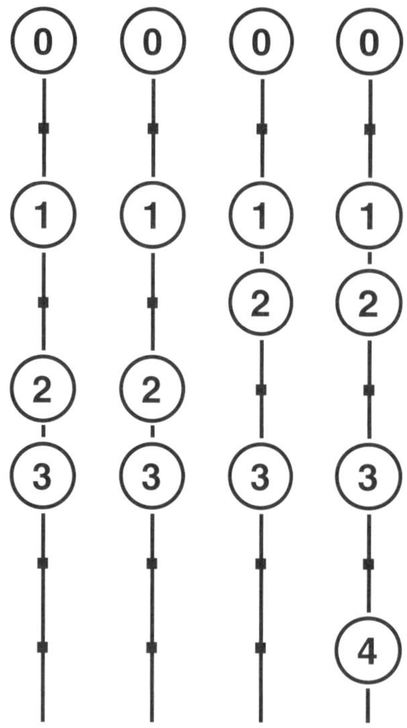

FIG. 2.3. C Major Frame with Open Strings G, D, and A

All the open strings are used. This can help with intonation as well as increasing fluidity. In this system, as in any playing situation, if you have a reason to use your fourth finger instead of the open strings, of course you should do so. But open strings are allowed in the exercises that follow, and in some cases, necessary.

Here, in standard notation, are seven major scales expressed as four-string frames. This way of playing a scale has also been called "extended range" or "expanded range." I prefer the word "frame," as it refers to the visual representation in the diagrams, and encourages the student to see all the notes of a key signature at once across the four strings. Each scale is played up to the highest scale tone in first position and back down, passing the starting note (unless it's the open C string), and continuing to the lowest available scale tone. Direction is reversed again, returning to the starting pitch. The resulting repeatable four-bar phrase is a good exercise for building fluidity in every key. By learning the exercise in all keys with efficient fingerings, you can create a "roadmap" for improvisation.

We'll start in the key of G major, and go around the circle of fifths.

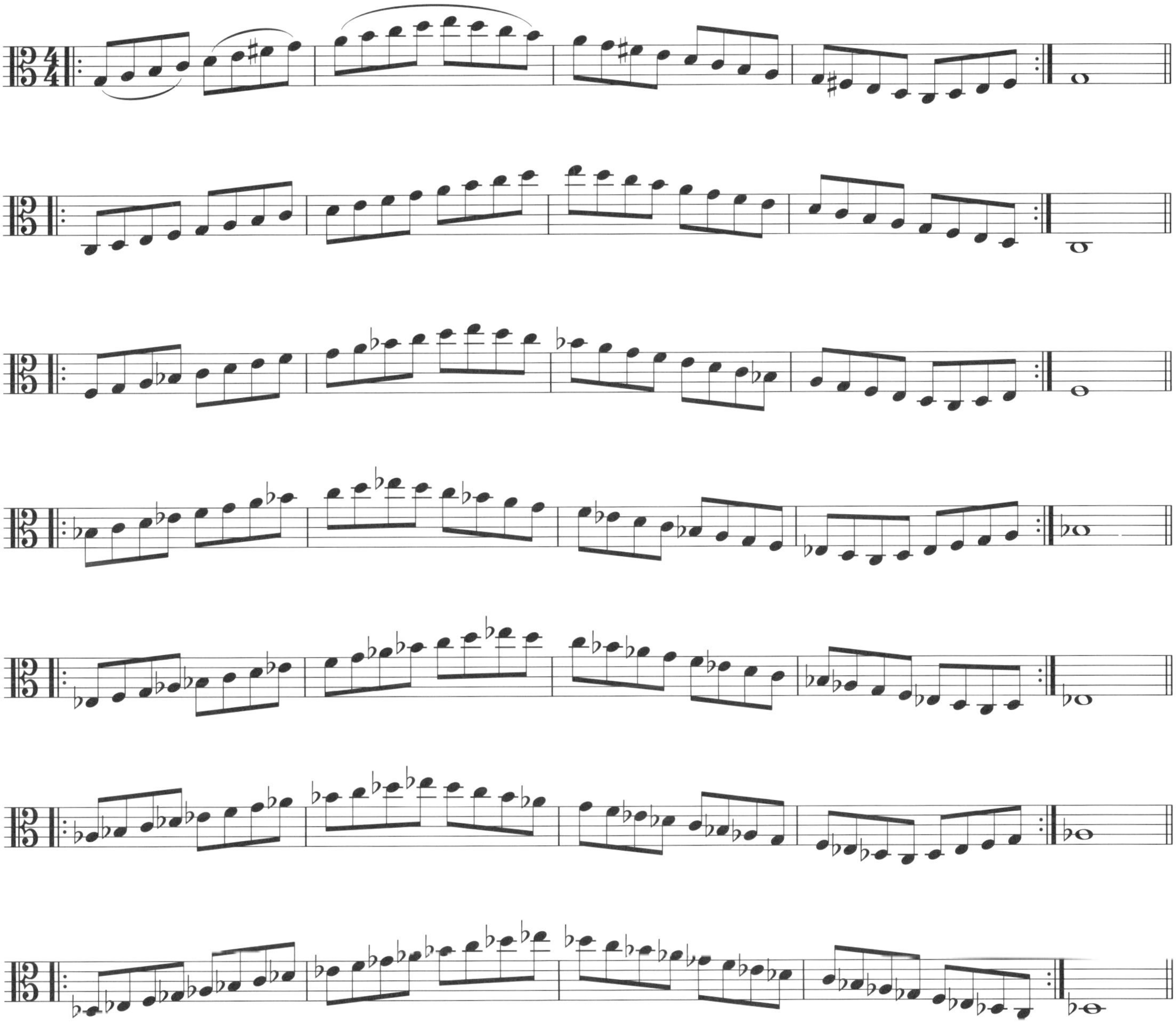

FIG. 2.4. Major Scales G through D♭ Around the Circle of Fifths

The seven scales above require no special instructions. They are in what you might consider the easiest or most convenient keys for the viola. One thing these keys have in common is that they all contain C♮, so the open C string is available. Notice that the availability of open strings began to decrease starting with the key of E♭.

CHAPTER 3

Four-String Frames and Five "Inconvenient" Keys

Of the seven scales presented at the end of chapter 2, D♭ was the last one with an open string available. It was the C string. If C♮ is in a scale, there will be a total of seventeen pitches played in the scale's four-string frame. If there are fewer than seventeen pitches in a scale played in this manner, the scale cannot be expressed as consecutive eighth notes in a four-bar phrase.

As we continue around the circle, adding another flat to the key signature, we arrive at the key of G♭. Without the open C string, there are only sixteen available pitches in the position. In order to maintain the four-bar phrase, the G♭ is played twice in bar 1 and in bar 2. It is not doubled again after that.

FIG. 3.1. G♭ Major with Doubled Root

The same pitches appear here (with the exception of the low C♯ and the addition of a high E♯), in the enharmonically equivalent key, F♯. Again, the root is doubled twice.

FIG. 3.2. F♯ Major with Doubled Root

For our purposes, there need be no distinction between these two scales in terms of fingering. You could play all but the lowest note of the G♭ scale starting with the third finger, and you could play all but the top note of the F♯ scale starting with the fourth finger. Technically, starting with the third finger on a G♭ scale would put you in second position for that key. Starting the F♯ scale with the fourth finger puts you in half position for that key. In this context, we will define "*half position*" simply as the lowest possible finger placements on the viola.

Figure 3.3 shows the two mutually exclusive fingerings for the G♭/F♯ pitch set side by side. Going forward, rather than naming these two positions by number, let's call them *low frame* and *high frame*. Tonic pitches are set white on black.

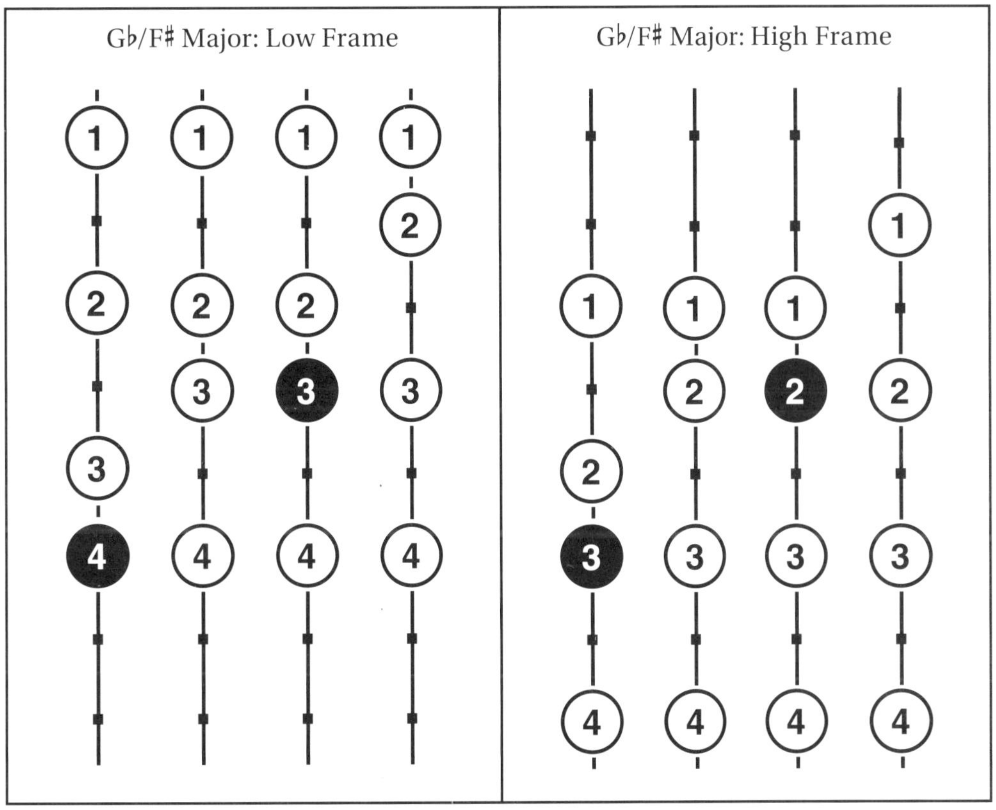

FIG. 3.3. G♭/F♯ Major: Low Frame and High Frame

The five key signatures presenting this type of fingering situation can be notated and diagrammed as *dual frames*. To play comfortably in those keys, awareness of the two fingerings is crucial, as is the ability to move between them efficiently.

Here are a couple of ways to move between the two frames. The fingerings above and below the staff are two different approaches. First play one, then try the other.

FIG. 3.4. G♭ Major Split Frame

Same-finger shifts, 1-1 or 2-2, are used in this example. The move can be executed between almost any pair of notes in the scale using the first, second, or third finger. When you shift between the low frame and the high frame, you are playing a split frame.

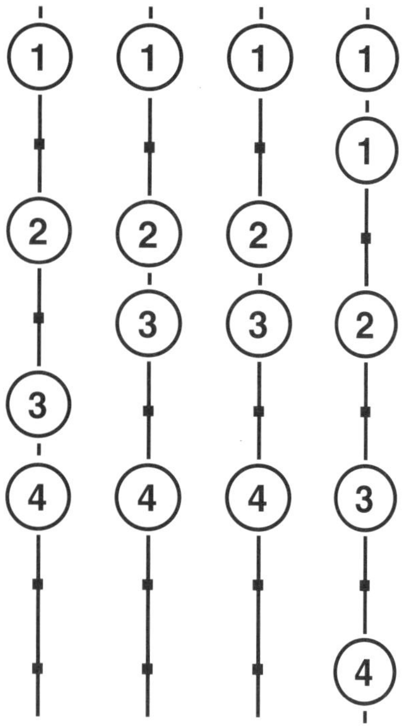

FIG. 3.5. G♭/F♯ Major Split-Frame Diagram

Next in the circle is B. Here are the three frames—low, high, and split—for the keys of C♭/B.

FIG. 3.6. C♭/B Major Dual and Split Frames

Now, we come to the E major scale. Just as open-string availability decreased after the key of E♭ in the first seven keys on the circle of fifths, we will now see three of them become available again in sequence in these last three keys. In the key of E, the open A string is available. In the split-frame fingering for this scale, the A string is used as a *pivot point* (it can exist in both frames) between the high frame on the A string and the low frame on the other three strings. A shift between the two positions executed while playing an open string is called a *pivot shift*.

As you execute the pivot shift while playing the open A, release the thumb slightly, and let your left hand "float" to the first-finger B. Some people with large hands prefer to leave the thumb in place and stretch the left hand between the two positions; if that feels comfortable, go for it. However, you are moving between half position and first position. They are very close, but not the same, and you may find the "floating shift" more efficient. Another option is to move the finger first and then let the thumb follow in a "crawl shift."

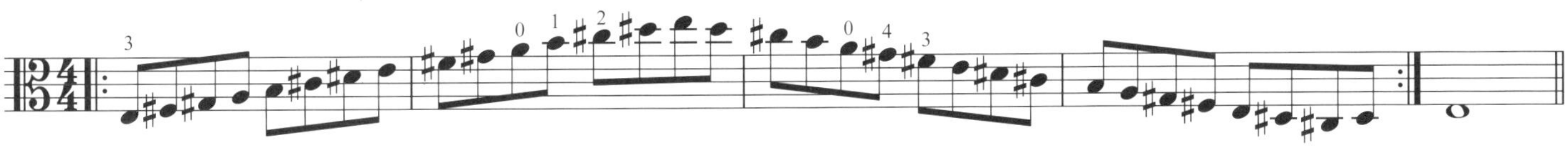

FIG. 3.7. E Major Split Frame

We'll look at the dual frames for these last three keys in a bit, but first, here are the split frames for the keys of A and D.

In the A major split frame, you'll go up the scale with the conventional fingering. On the way down, make the pivot shift around the open D string. Then, as you ascend from the low C♯, you stay in the low frame. If you observe the repeat, you'll be in the low frame on the G string during the first two beats of bar 1, moving to the more familiar high frame after open D. If not, you'll end on second-finger A.

Since there are potentially two open strings in this scale, you have two options for the pivot shift: around the D string or the A string.

FIG. 3.8. A Major Split Frame

In D major, it's a similar situation, but there are now three available open strings, so three options for the pivot move back and forth between the high and low frames. (The A-string pivot option would be the same as in figure 3.8, the A scale.)

FIG. 3.9. D Major Split Frame

The high and low (dual) frames of E, A, and D should also be played. If they feel awkward at first, remember that all of these fingerings combine familiar single-string frames.

In the high E frame in figure 3.10, the frame on the C string (including the D♯ in bar four) is hww. On the G string, it is www; on the D and A strings, wwh.

In the low frame, notice that the fingering is the same as F major, until you get to the A string. Before you try this fingering, play an F major scale with no open strings up to A. Now, move your hand back a half step and play an E major scale. Not difficult. On the A string, even though your first finger is not used, it should rest on the string behind the second finger forming the hww single-string frame.

FIG. 3.10. E Major High and Low Frames

Here are the high and low frames for A major.

FIG. 3.11. A Major High and Low Frames

The low frame might feel a little weird. Let's take a look at its diagram.

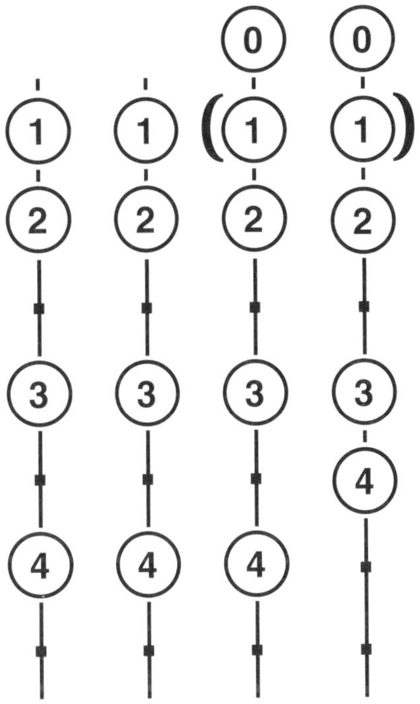

FIG. 3.12. Low A Four-String Frame Diagram

The first finger rests on the D and A strings, but E♭ and B♭ are not played. As you can see, there are hww frames on the C, G, and D strings, and the hwh frame on the A string. You should get used to that one. It will come in handy as you advance to scales such as diminished and jazz melodic minor.

Lastly, here are high and low frames for D major. The high frame is very familiar, but not the low frame.

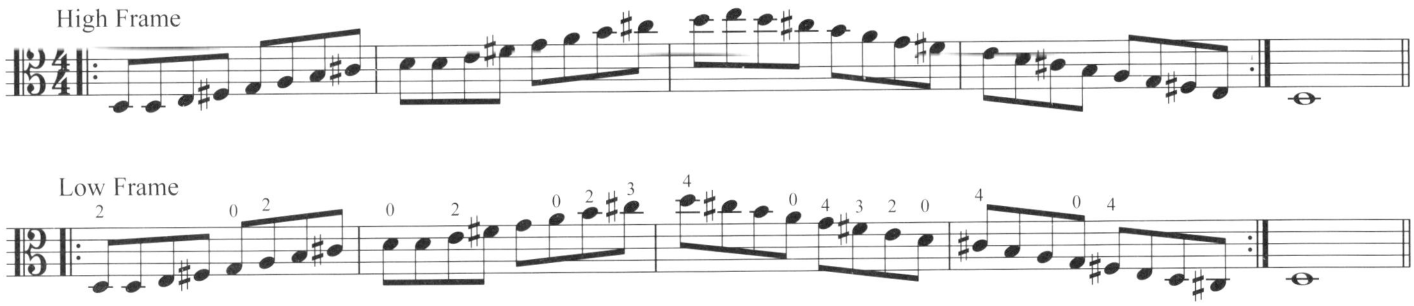

FIG. 3.13. D Major High and Low Frames

Here's the diagram. Again, first fingers in parentheses are lightly placed, but the corresponding notes are not sounded.

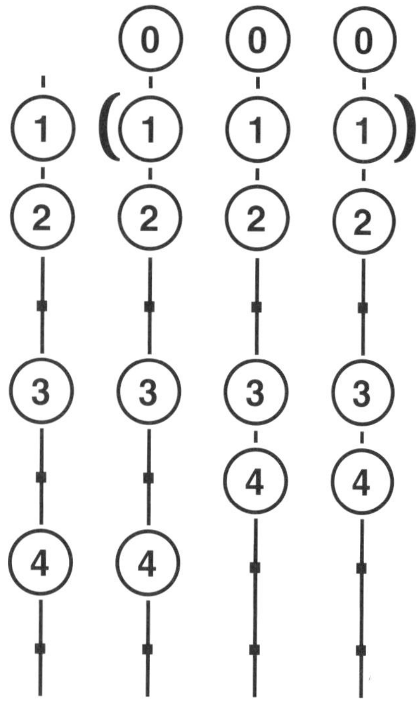

FIG. 3.14. Low D Four-String Frame Diagram

Why on earth would anyone want to finger a D major scale like that? The first finger has nothing to do on three of the strings, and the fourth finger is playing a G and a D that should be played with the third finger. What's the deal?

Here's the deal: The unplayed first fingers can be used as chromatic passing and approach tones in between the open strings and second fingers.

FIG. 3.15. Bebop Line

That is a bebop line that might be played over an A7 chord in the key of D. In that key, this kind of jazz vocabulary is accessed very comfortably in half position with the use of open strings.

Why Is Everything in First (and Half) Position?

It is important to be completely comfortable in the lower register of all keys and to remove the barriers to fluency created by a lack of awareness of the value of half position in the sharp keys. After that's done, of course, the exercises throughout this book can be played in fixed positions moving up the neck (see dual frames in appendix A), and eventually in three octaves.

CHAPTER 4

Seven Modes and Seven Chords

The scales in the preceding pages are all major scales. As you know, every major key and scale has a relative minor key and scale. The relative minor of C major is A minor, the relative minor of G major is E minor, etc. What the orchestra teacher might not have told you is that there are five other "relatives" of every major scale. These relatives are called "modes." Their names come from ancient Greece: Ionian (same as the major scale), Dorian, Phrygian, Lydian, Mixolydian, Aeolian (same as natural minor, the relative minor of the major scale), and Locrian.

Take a look at the C major scale and its six relative modes. They can be played quite easily on the white keys of a keyboard instrument.

C Ionian (Major)

D Dorian

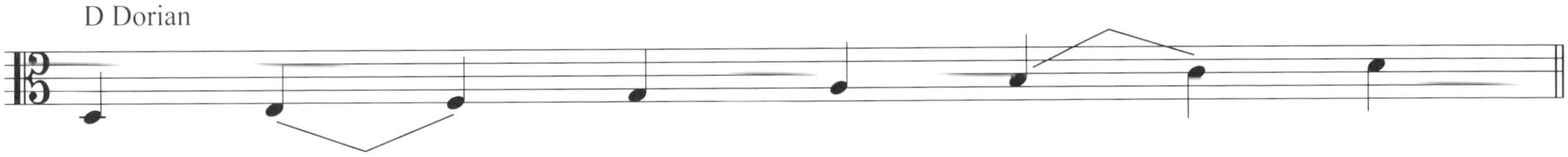

E Phrygian

F Lydian

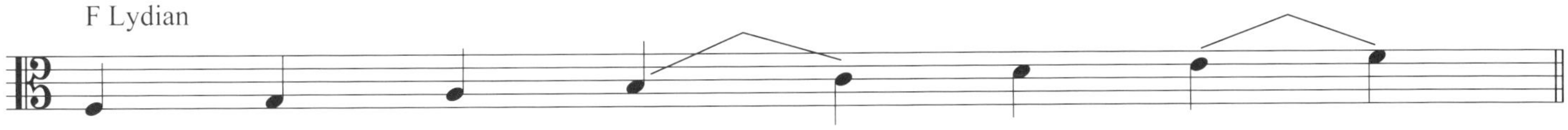

G Mixolydian

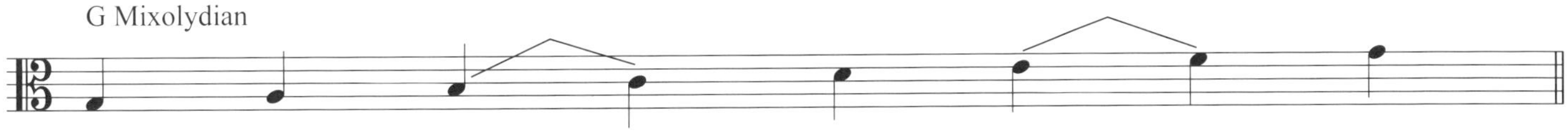

A Aeolian (Natural Minor)

B Locrian

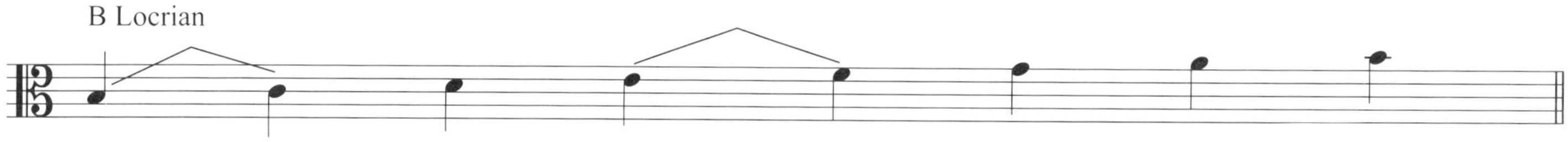

FIG. 4.1. The Seven Modes

In the context of jazz improvisation, modes are sometimes called "chord scales." This is because improvisers associate these scales with chords. You could say that scales can generate chords, or the reverse—that certain chords suggest certain scales to the improviser.

More than one chord with C as the root can be constructed using the notes in a C major scale, but for the sake of simplicity, we'll start with 1, 3, 5, and 7. When C, E, G, and B are stacked up, a C major 7 chord (CMaj7) is generated. CMaj7 is a C major triad with an added major 7.

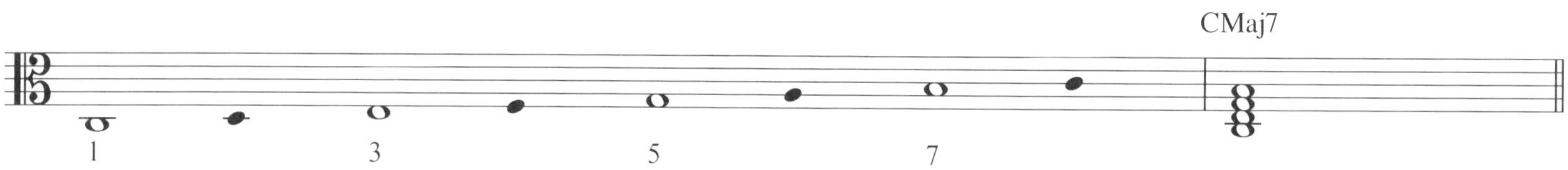

FIG. 4.2. C Major Scale and CMaj7

When the scale tones become chord tones, their names in the chord are root (1), third (3), fifth (5), and seventh (7).

The chord symbol "CMaj7" appears above the notated chord. In jazz notation, chord symbols appear above melodies to indicate the harmonic progression ("chord progression" or "chord changes") of a tune. When players see that chord symbol, they know that the notes in the C major scale can be used to construct an improvised melody.

Here's an example of a jazz line (or "lick") that might be created by a soloist who encounters the chord symbol in a progression.

FIG. 4.3. CMaj7 Jazz Lick

All the notes in the C major scale are used at least once in this lick. Notice that the first six notes in the melody in figure 4.3 are the notes in the CMaj7 chord. Playing chord notes sequentially ("arpeggiating" chords) is an important part of jazz improvisation.

Although the scales discussed here provide an essential framework for improvising on chord progressions, eventually, they provide a point of departure for more advanced melodic ideas. Here's a lick based in the C major scale framework that uses four notes that aren't in the scale.

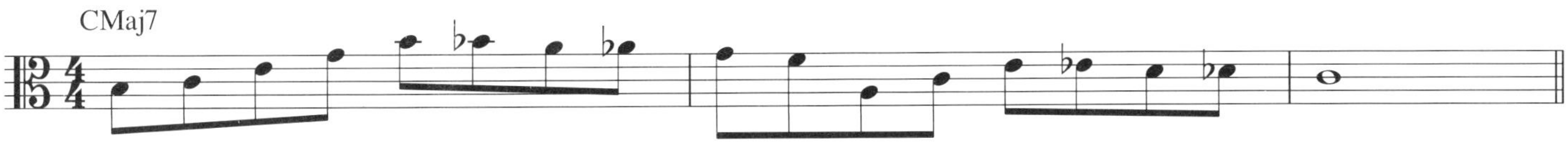

FIG. 4.4. CMaj7 Jazz Lick with Passing Tones

The non-scale tones B♭, A♭, E♭, and D♭ are passing tones. They are chromatic connections between notes that are in the scale. This is a common device in both classical and jazz music. Of course you are encouraged to explore such ideas, eventually, but be mindful of the importance of establishing a solid diatonic foundation. A good grasp of the materials and strategies outlined in this system will make for a more organized approach as you progress.

Let's examine the seven modes again, in the key of C, and consider some chords they generate. CMaj7 and Dmi7 are constructed using 1-3-5-7 from Ionian and Dorian, respectively.

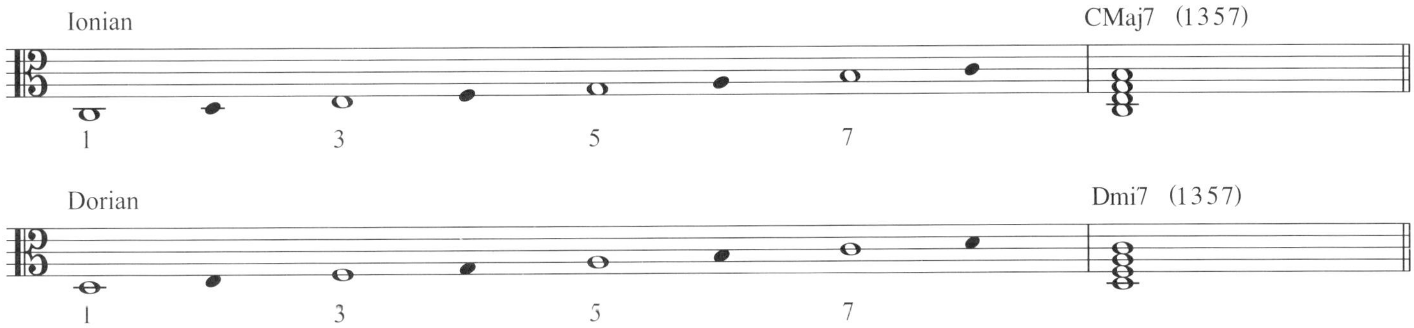

FIG. 4.5. Ionian and Dorian in the Key of C

In the case of the Phrygian mode, if we used 1-3-5-7, the resulting chord would be Emi7. So, we avoid duplication of the mi7 chord type (which we used for Dorian) and better express the "Phrygian sound" by using 1-2-4-5. You won't see a lot of sus(♭9) chords in jazz lead sheets, but learning this intervallic "shape" (half step, major third, whole step) will turn out to be very important! The second degree of the scale is called ♭9 when used in a chord.

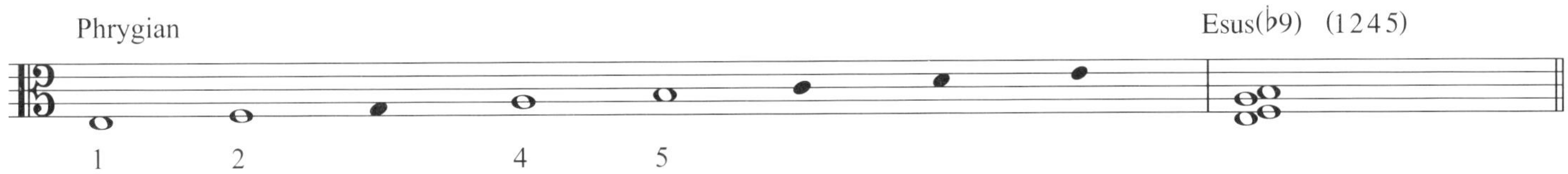

FIG. 4.6. Phrygian in the Key of C

In the Lydian chord, scale degree 4 replaces the 5 of the chord. Notice that the Lydian chord contains the same four pitches as the Phrygian chord.

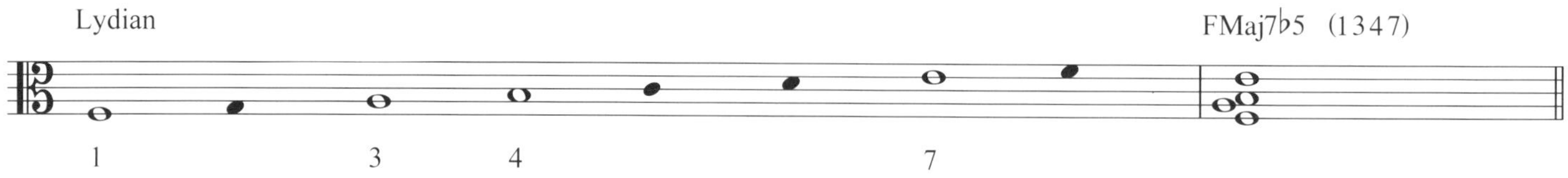

FIG. 4.7. Lydian in the Key of C

The dominant 7, or simply "7," chord is built using 1-3-5-7 from the Mixolydian mode.

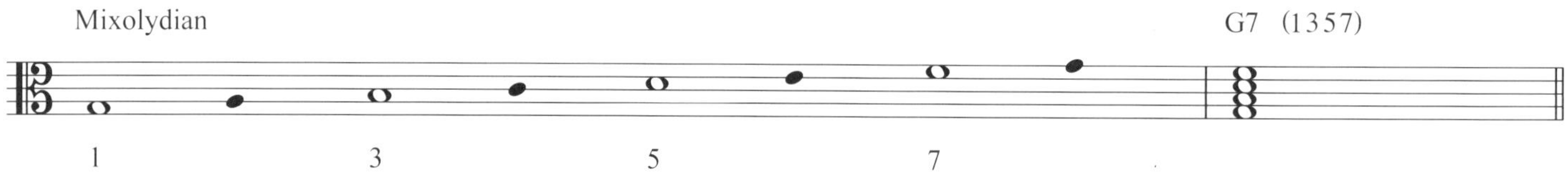

FIG. 4.8. Mixolydian in the Key of C

Again, in Aeolian, using the F (the low 6) in the Ami♭6 chord instead of G (the 7) avoids duplication, and better expresses the character of the mode.

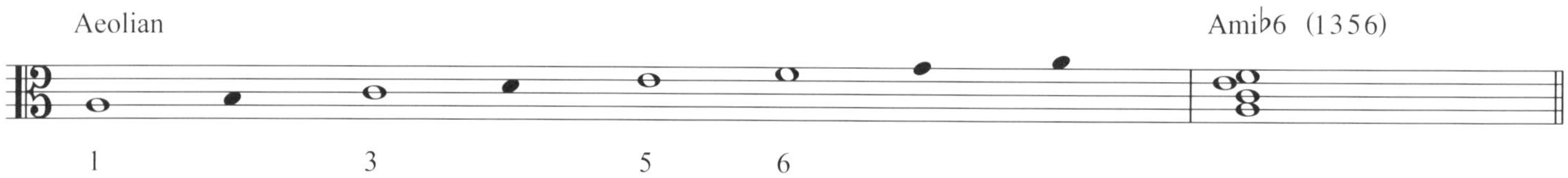

FIG. 4.9. Aeolian in the Key of C

And lastly, from the Locrian mode, 1-3-5-7 produces the Bmi7♭5 (aka half-diminished chord).

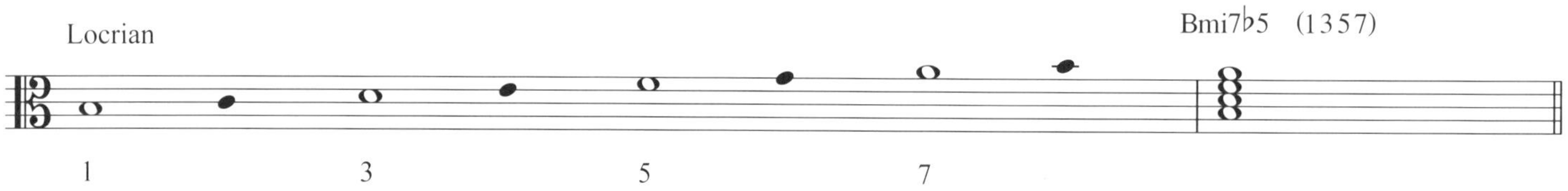

FIG. 4.10. Locrian in the Key of C

It's a good idea to commit this ordering of the seven modes to memory. Remember, you can find these modes on the white keys of the piano any time you need to, just by playing C to C, D to D, E to E, etc. The initials of the modes in this order produce this acronym: IDPLMAL. It has too many consonants in a row to be much good until you put some memorable words to it:

I Don't **P**lay **L**ike **M**y **A**unt **L**iza.

Here's another modes mnemonic, with thanks and a tip of the "scale nerd" hat to Roxanne Young.

"**I D**on't **P**articularly **L**ike **M**odes." — **A**braham **L**incoln

CHAPTER 5

Mode/Arpeggio Exercises in a Key

Here is a system of exercises in which the seven modes of each major scale are played as four-string frames, followed by the associated arpeggios. By starting on and returning to each successive pitch in a scale, you will play all six of its "relatives," and hear the seven possible tonal centers present in the scale. Practice the exercises one at a time, slowly at first, building velocity gradually. They should eventually be played as fast as possible without sacrificing accuracy. Play four or eight notes to a bow, and in the 9/8 arpeggios, three or nine to a bow. Once you are comfortable with the routine, experiment with other bowings. Fingerings appear where needed to indicate shifts between first and half (and occasionally second) position. Appendix A has a chart of all the major-key frame diagrams, organized for easy reference.

The open strings indicated in the frame diagrams are suggested as a means to maximize facility/fluidity in navigating a given key signature. Again, if you have the impulse to use a fourth finger instead, for any reason, feel free to do so in the first nine keys. After that, you'll need open strings for pivot shifts. You'll see lots of "4-0-1" and "1-0-4" moves.

Why Are Some Arpeggios in 9/8 and Others in 4/4?

It depends on the number of available notes (nine or ten) in a frame. There are a few split-frame arpeggios that change position, but for ease of playing, most of them stay in the low frame even when the corresponding scale has a split frame. To create an even, repeatable phrase when a total of ten notes are available, the arpeggio is in 9/8; when nine notes are available, it's in 4/4.

MODES OF G MAJOR

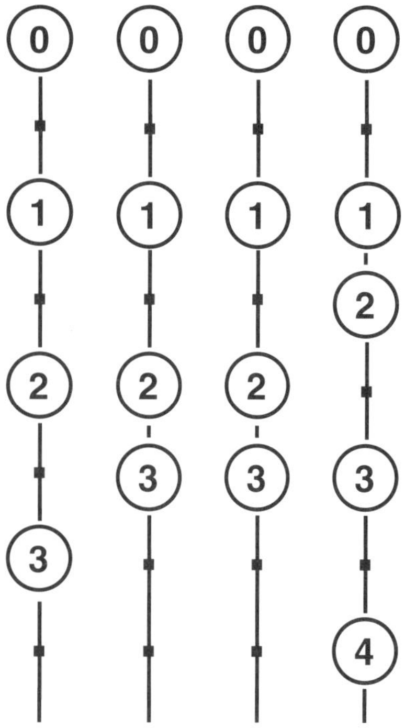

G Ionian

GMaj7

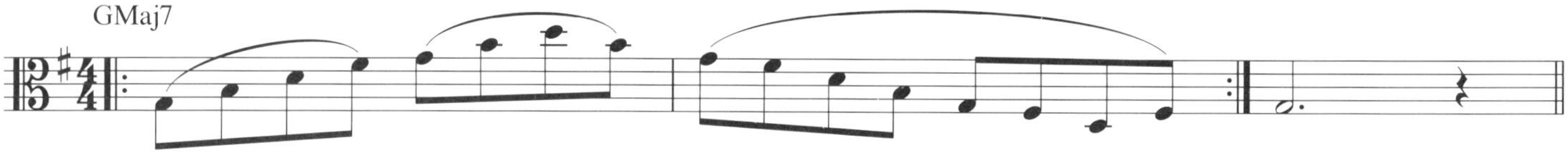

A Dorian

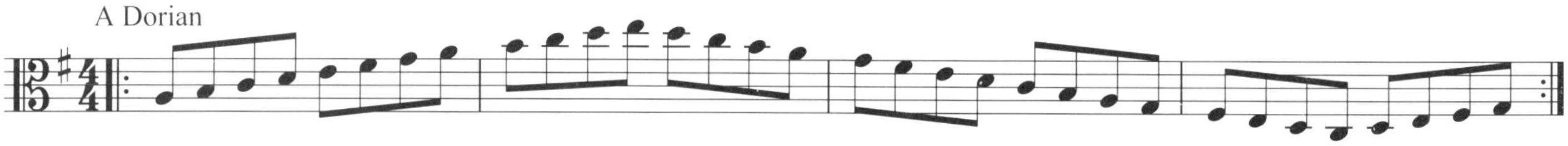

♩ = ♩.
or
♪ = ♪

Ami7

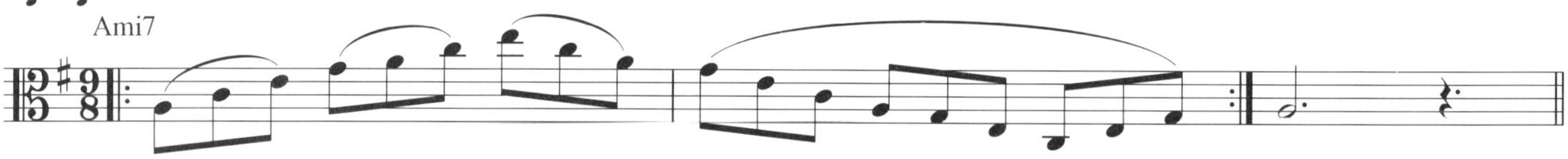

B Phrygian

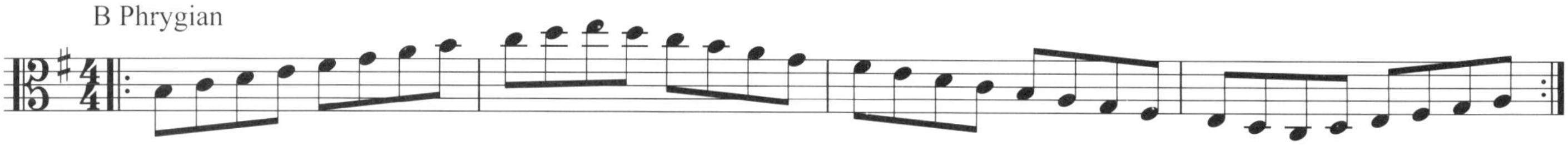

Bsus(♭9)

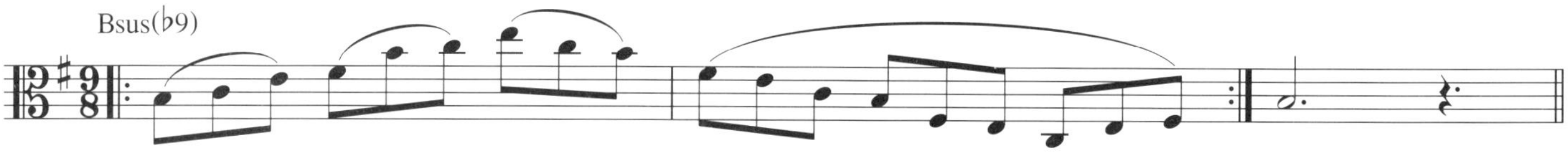

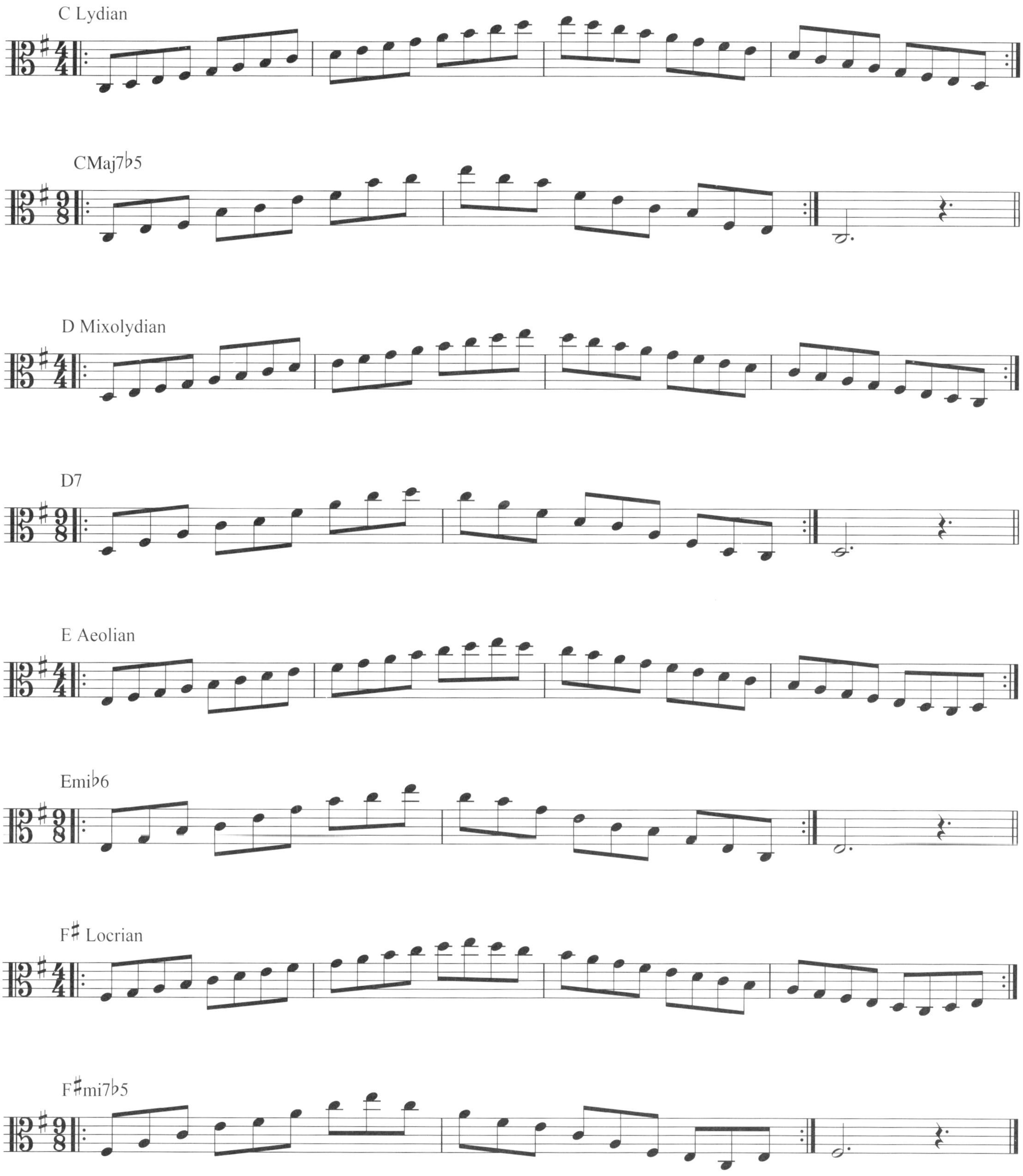

FIG. 5.1. Modes of G Major

MODES OF C MAJOR

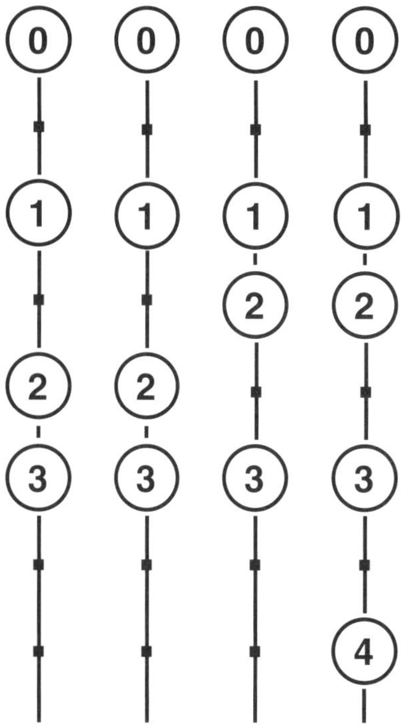

C Ionian

♩ = ♩.
or
♪ = ♪

CMaj7

D Dorian

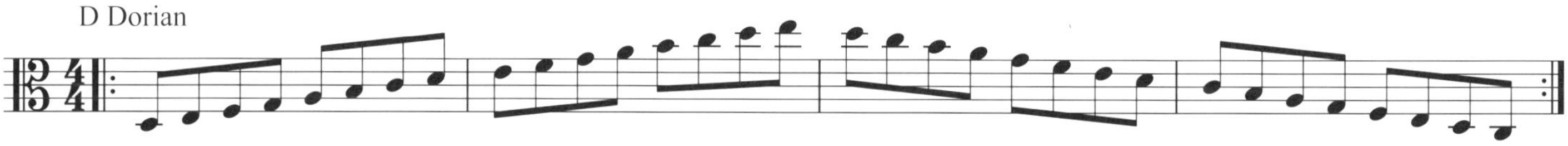

Dmi7

E Phrygian

Esus(♭9)

F Lydian

FMaj7♭5

G Mixolydian

G7

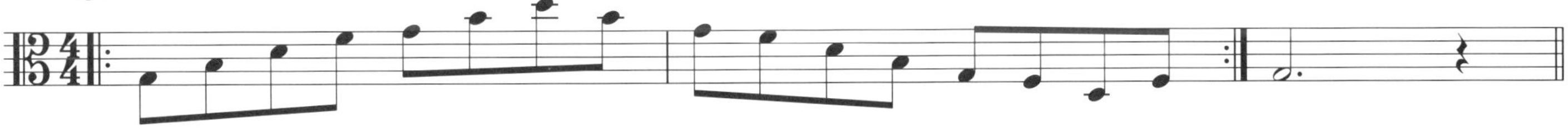

A Aeolian

Ami♭6

B Locrian

Bmi7♭5

FIG. 5.2. Modes of C Major

MODES OF F MAJOR

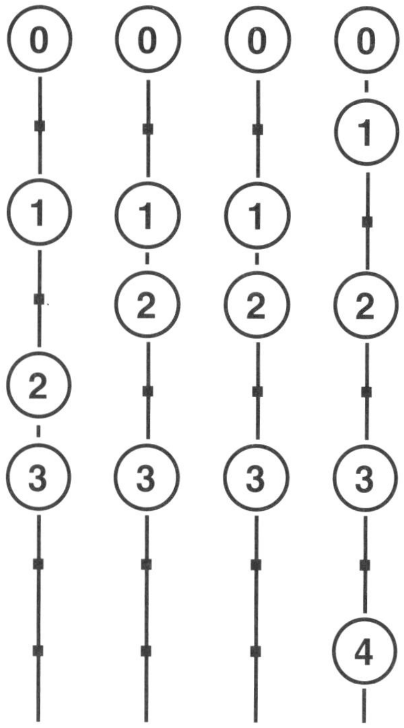

F Ionian

♩ = ♩.
or
♪ = ♪

FMaj7

G Dorian

Gmi7

A Phrygian

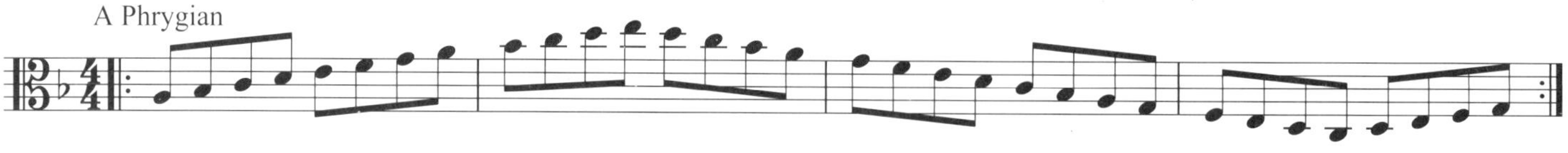

Asus(♭9)

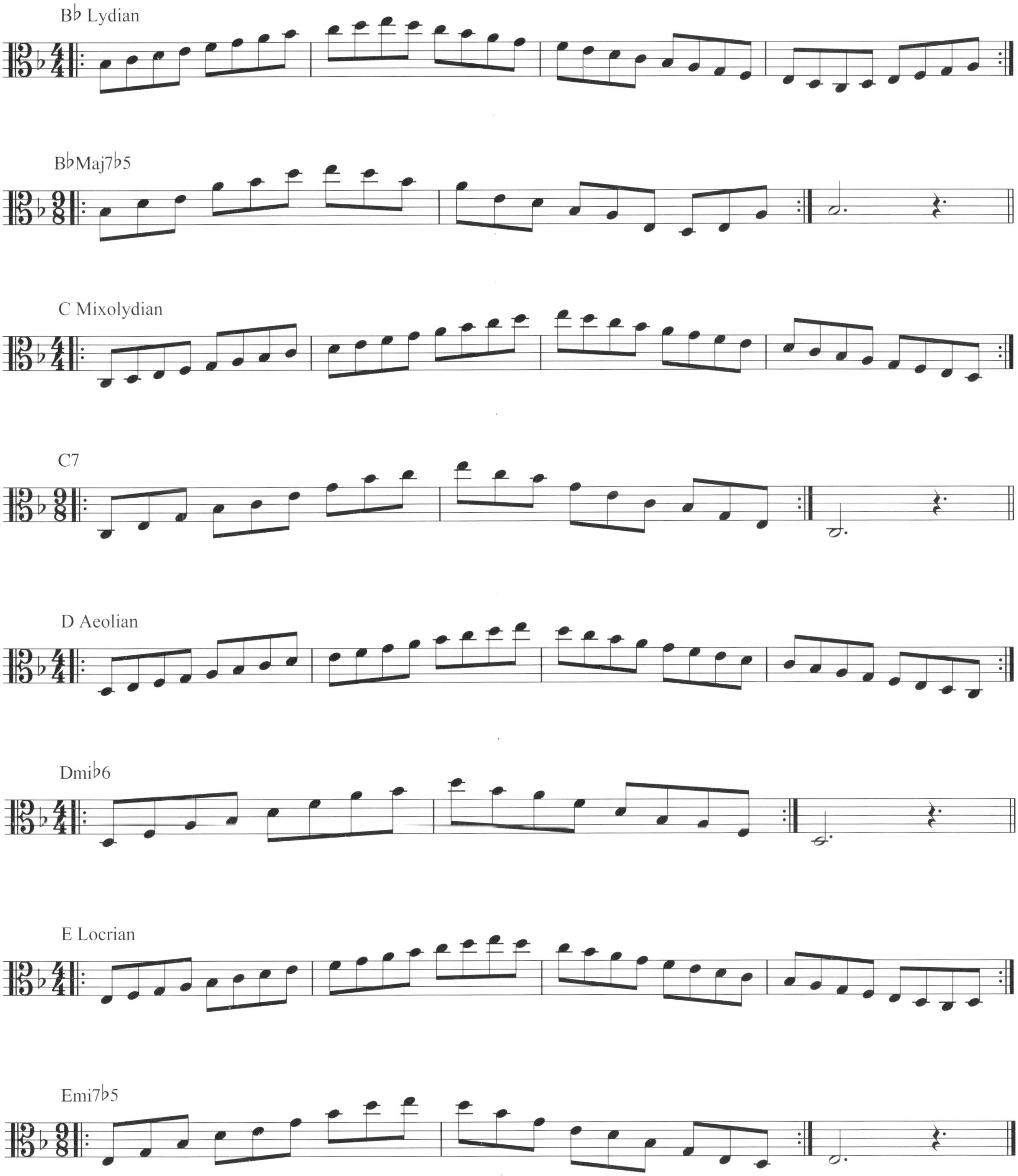

FIG. 5.3. Modes of F Major

MODES OF B♭ MAJOR

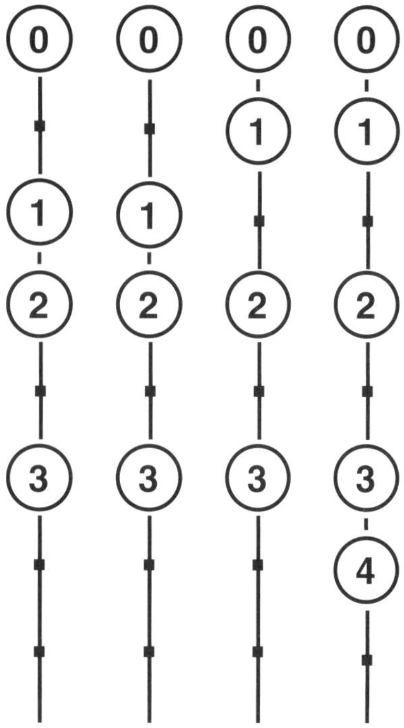

B♭ Ionian

B♭Maj7

C Dorian

♩ = ♩.
or
♪ = ♪

Cmi7

D Phrygian

Dsus(♭9)

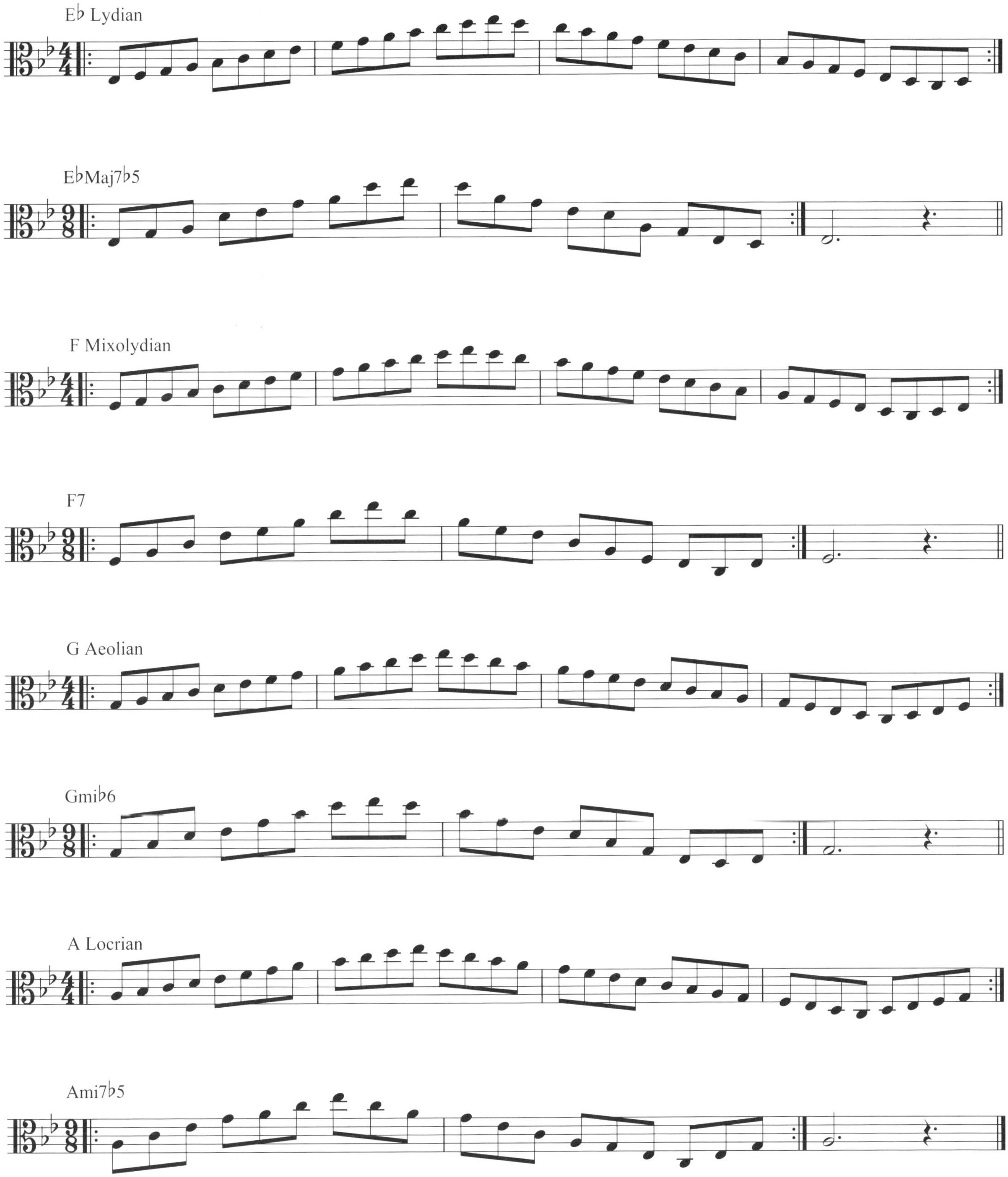

FIG. 5.4. Modes of B♭ Major

MODES OF E♭ MAJOR

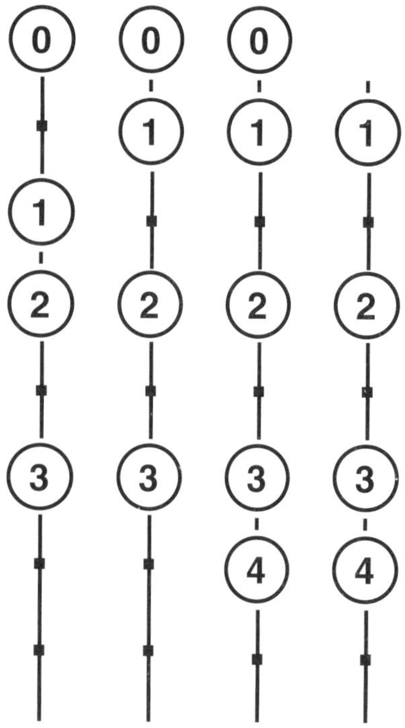

E♭ Ionian

E♭Maj7

F Dorian

♩ = ♩.
or
♪ = ♪

Fmi7

G Phrygian

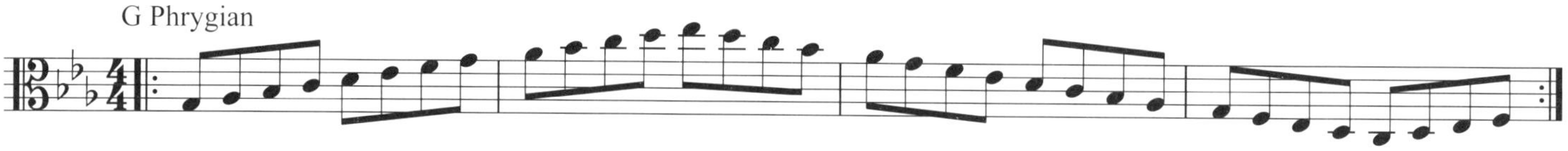

Gsus(♭9)

A♭ Lydian

A♭Maj7♭5

B♭ Mixolydian

B♭7

C Aeolian

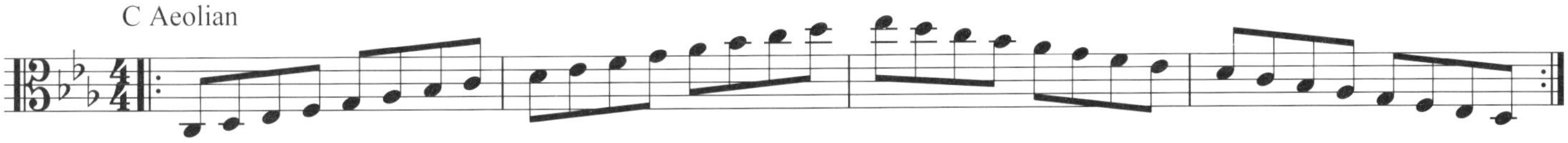

Cmi♭6

D Locrian

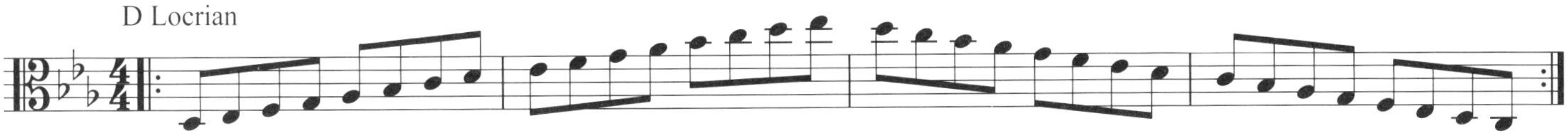

Dmi7♭5

FIG. 5.5. Modes of E♭ Major

MODES OF A♭ MAJOR

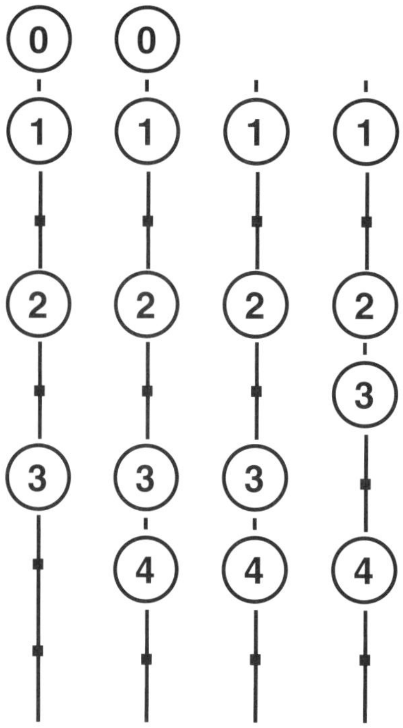

A♭ Ionian

♩ = ♩.
or
♪ = ♪

A♭Maj7

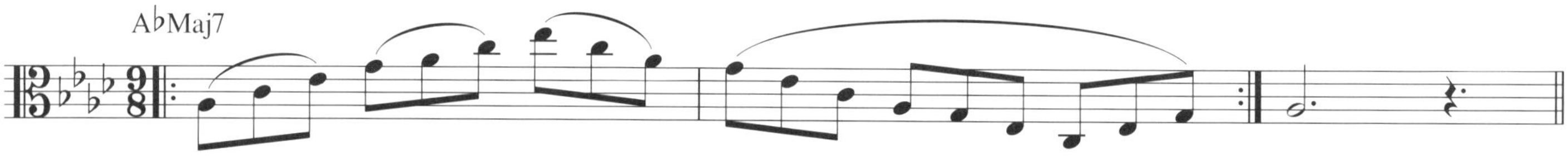

B♭ Dorian

B♭mi7

C Phrygian

Csus(♭9)

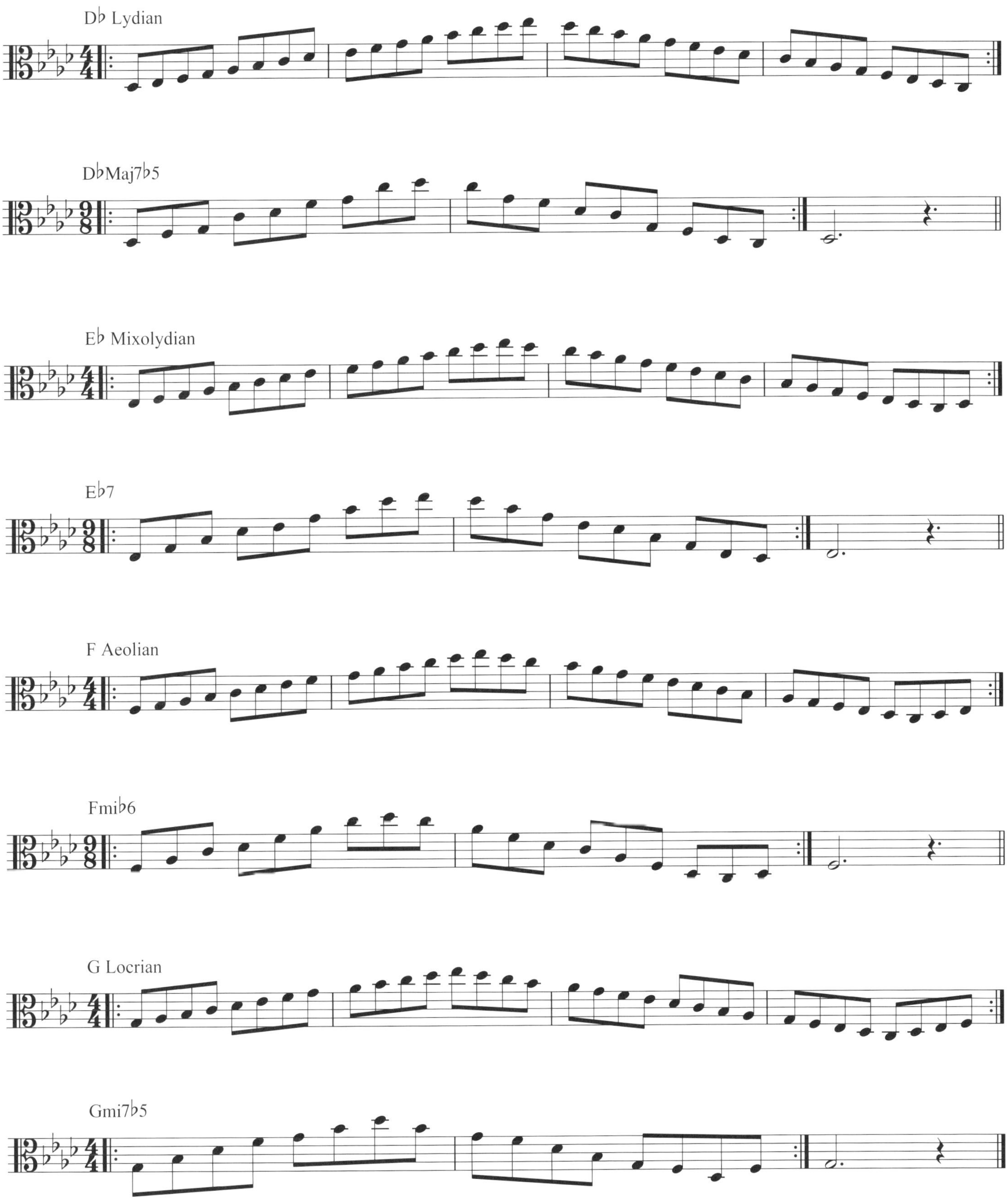

FIG. 5.6. Modes of A♭ Major

MODES OF D♭ MAJOR

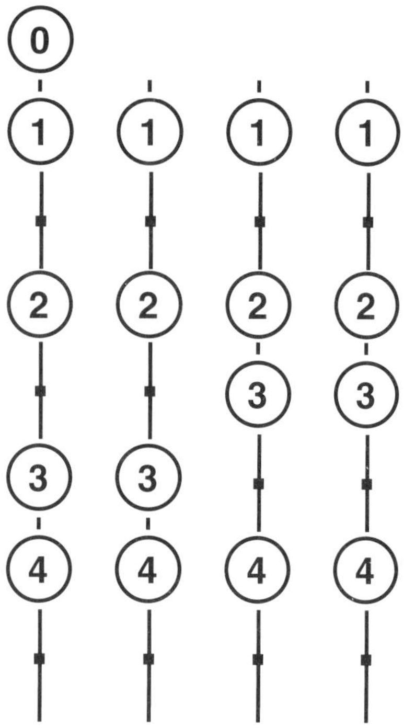

D♭ Ionian

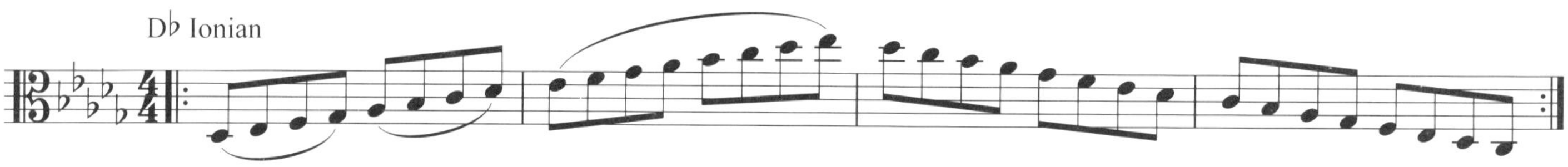

♩ = ♩.
or
♪ = ♪

D♭Maj7

E♭ Dorian

E♭mi7

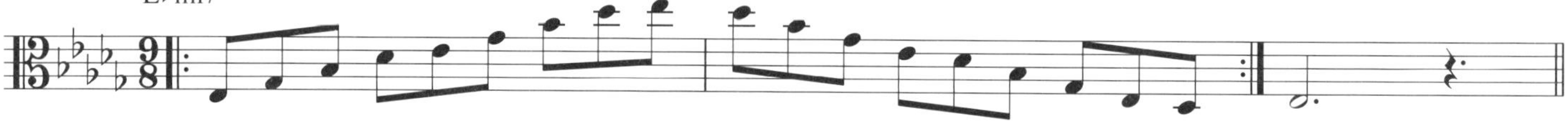

F Phrygian

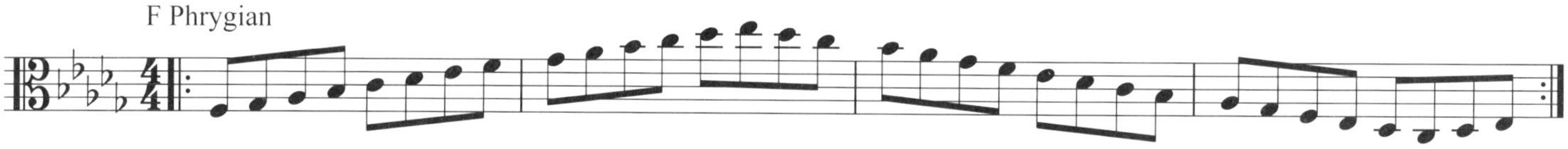

Fsus(♭9)

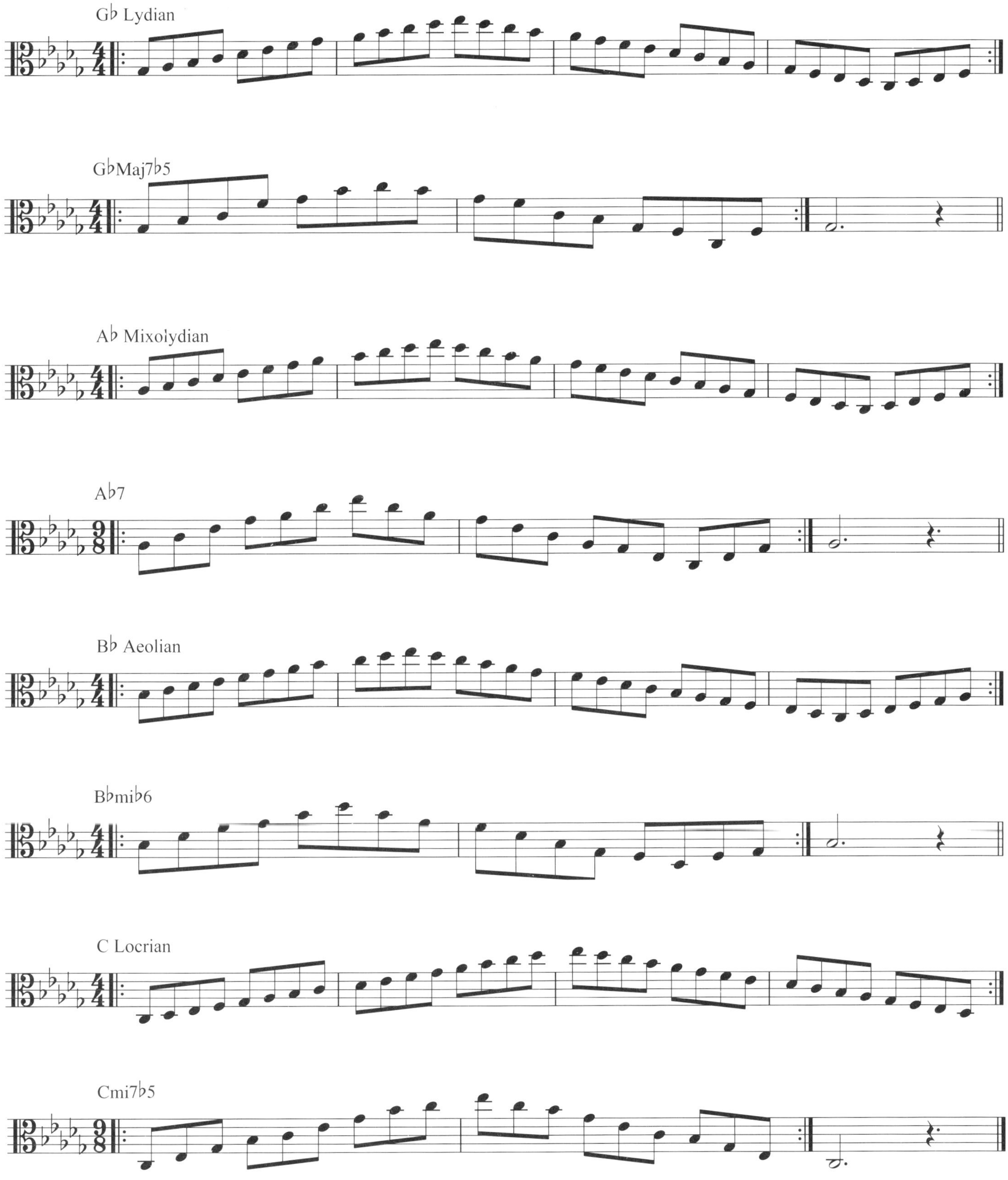

FIG. 5.7. Modes of D♭ Major

MODES OF G♭ MAJOR

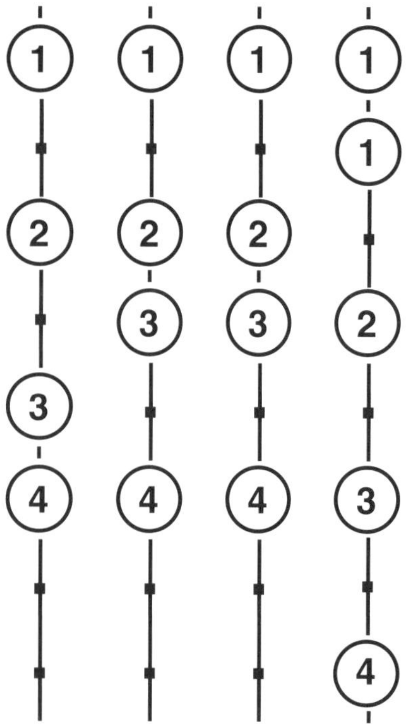

As we press on into the "inconvenient" keys, the fingerings for the Ionian mode should be applied to each mode in the key. Resist the impulse to disregard them if they seem unconventional. "Reminders" appear throughout the exercises, along with a variety of other fingering possibilities. Explore every option and combination of options to build the ability to navigate spontaneously between frames. In the interest of simplicity and velocity, some arpeggios have only nine notes when a tenth note is within reach via an alternate fingering. For a list of those "expandable" arpeggios, see Appendix B.

G♭ Ionian

G♭Maj7

A♭ Dorian

A♭mi7

B♭ Phrygian

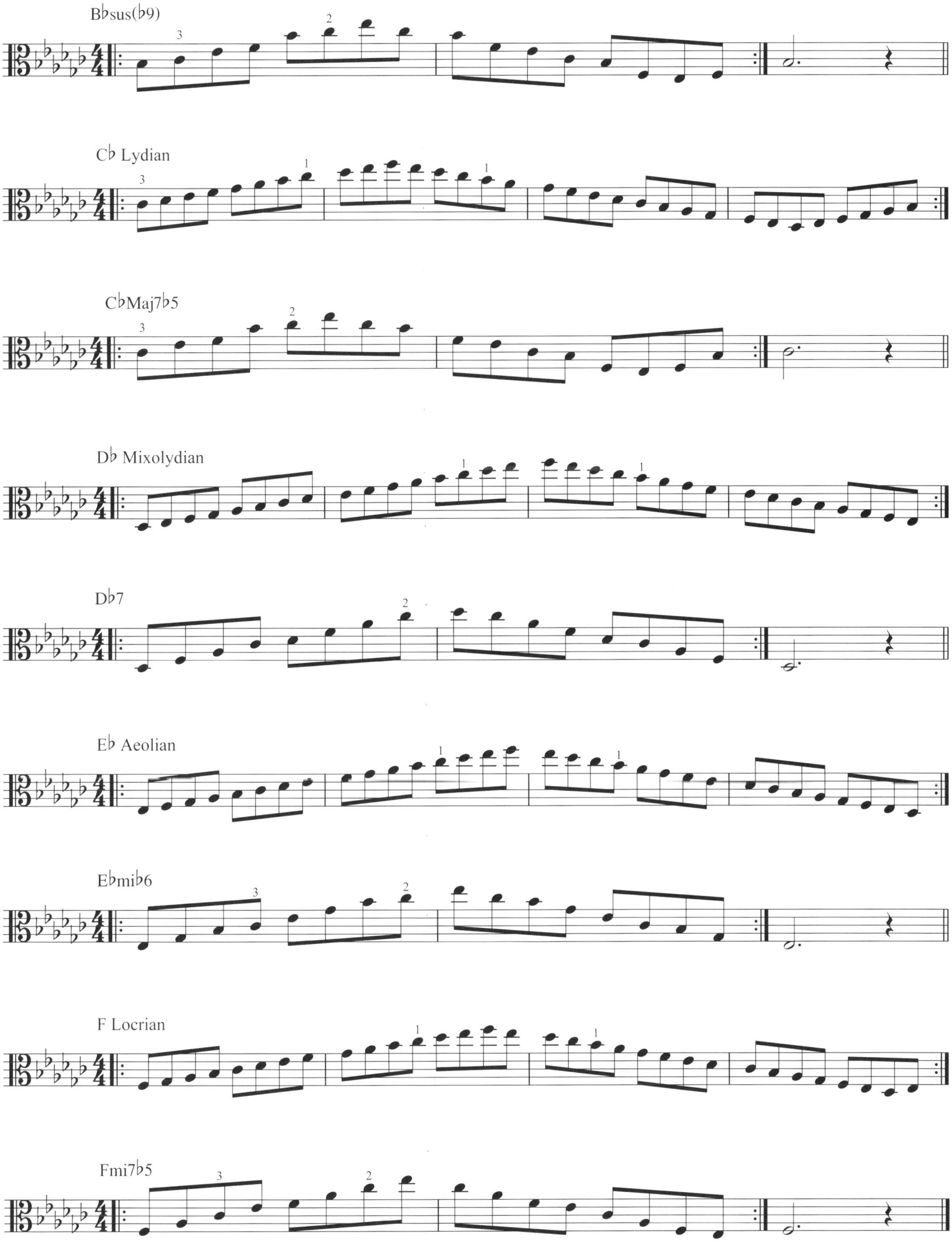

FIG. 5.8. Modes of G♭ Major

MODES OF B MAJOR

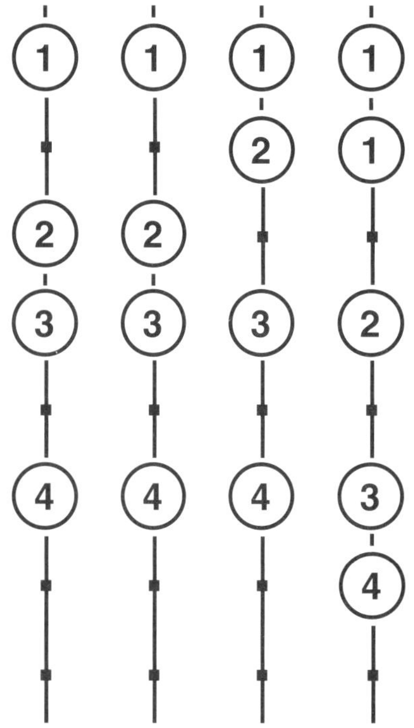

B Ionian

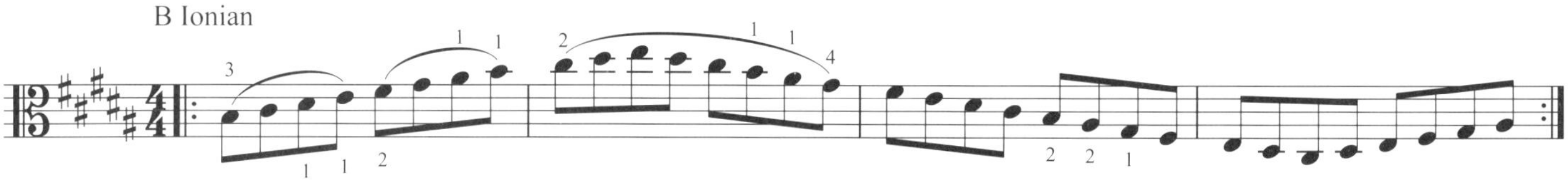

BMaj7

C♯ Dorian

Fingerings Simile...

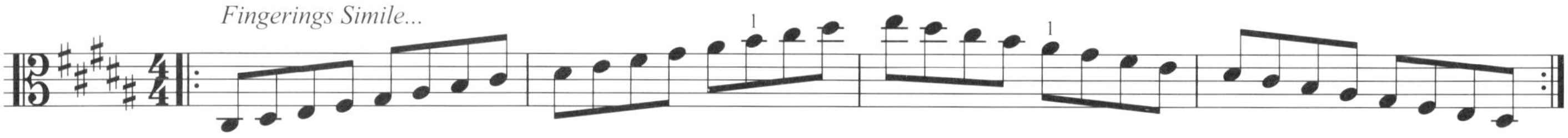

C♯mi7

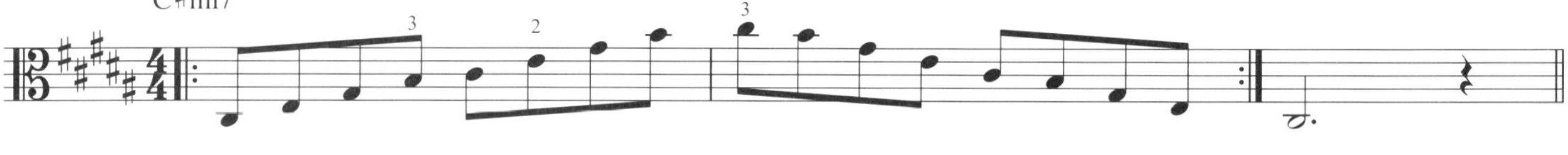

D♯ Phrygian

D♯sus(♭9)

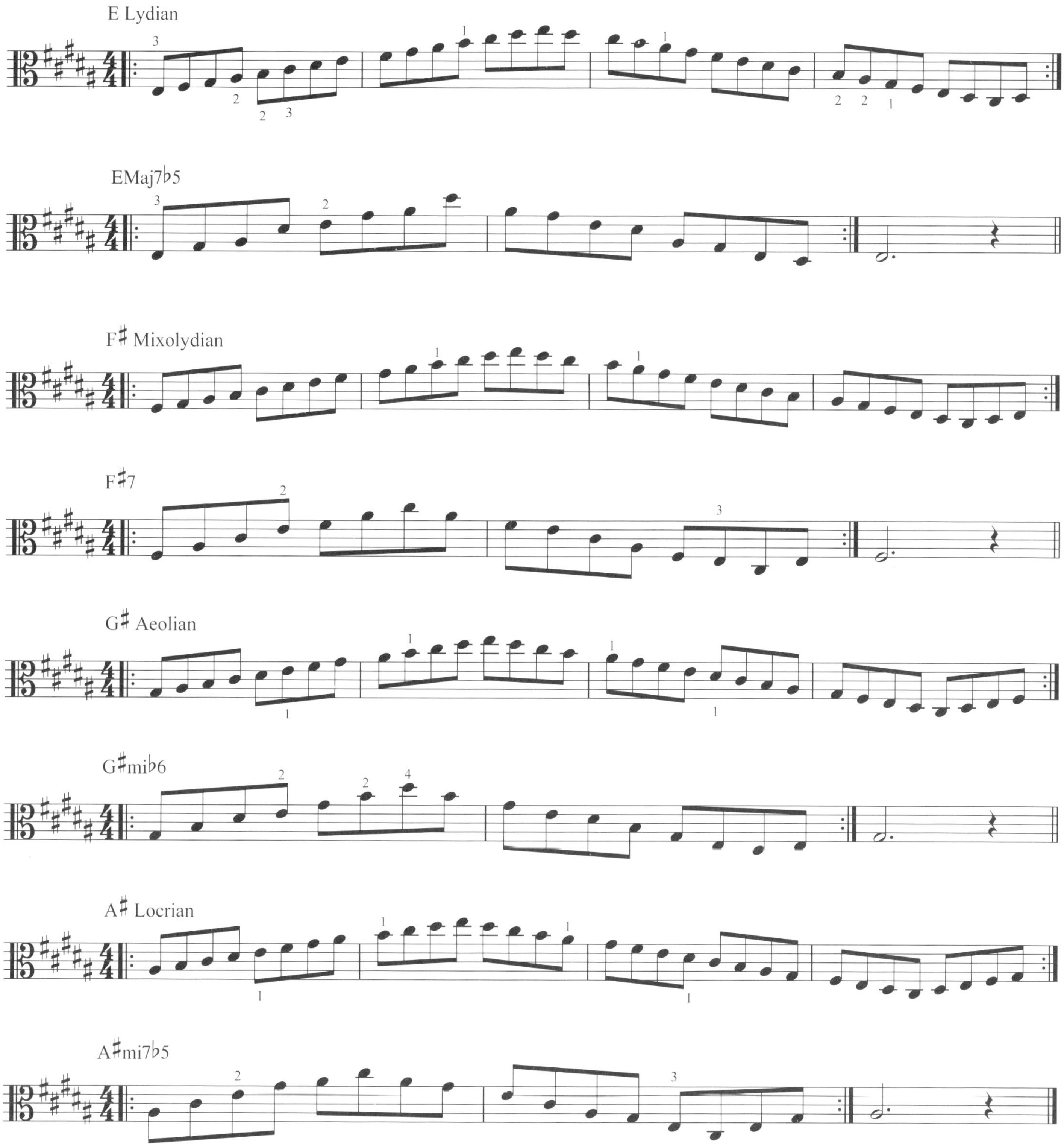

FIG. 5.9. Modes of B Major

MODES OF E MAJOR

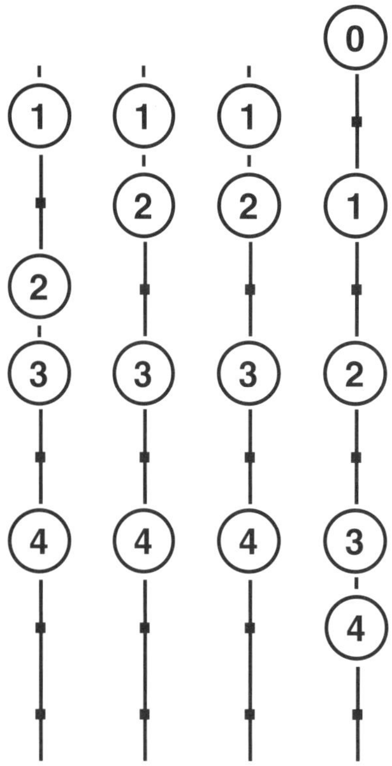

E Ionian

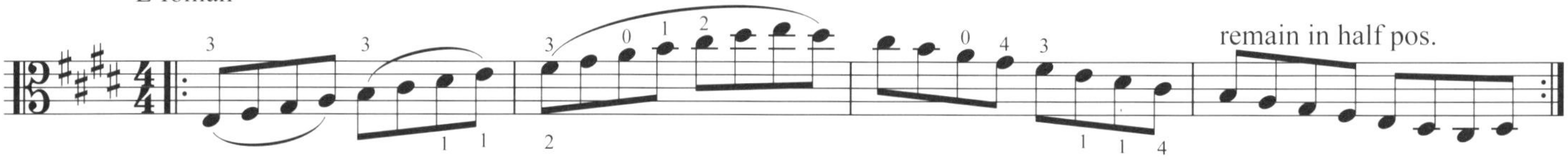

EMaj7

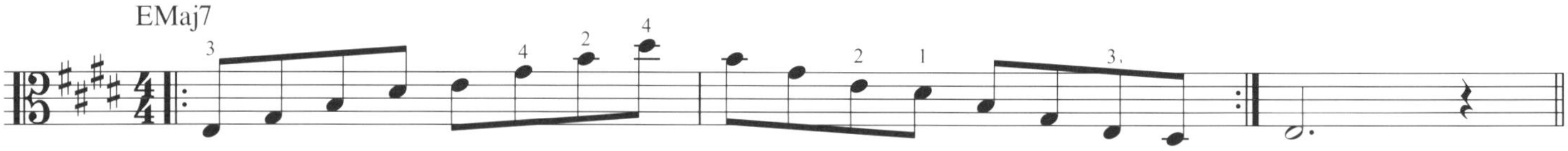

F♯ Dorian

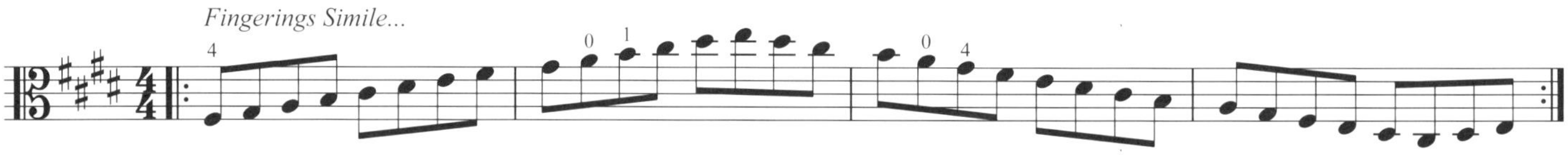

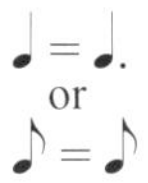

F♯mi7

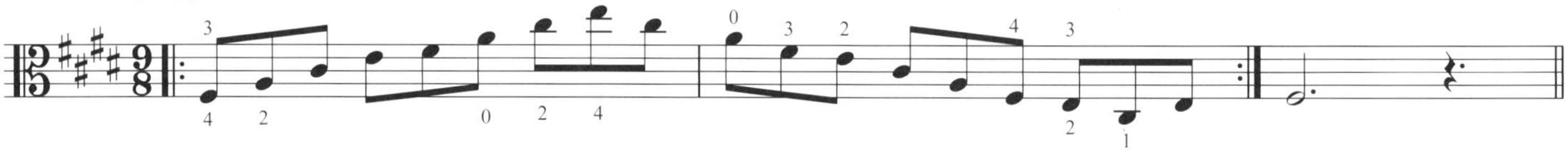

G♯ Phrygian

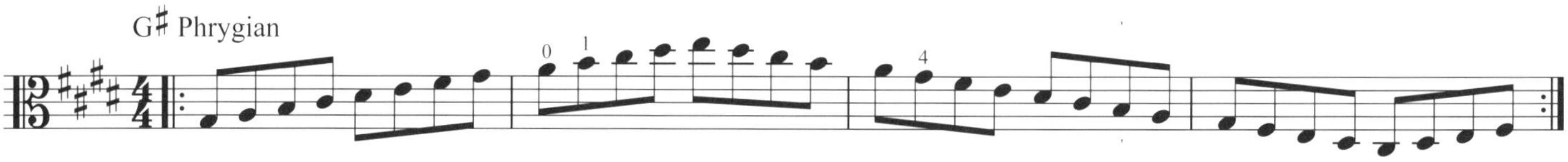

G♯sus(♭9)

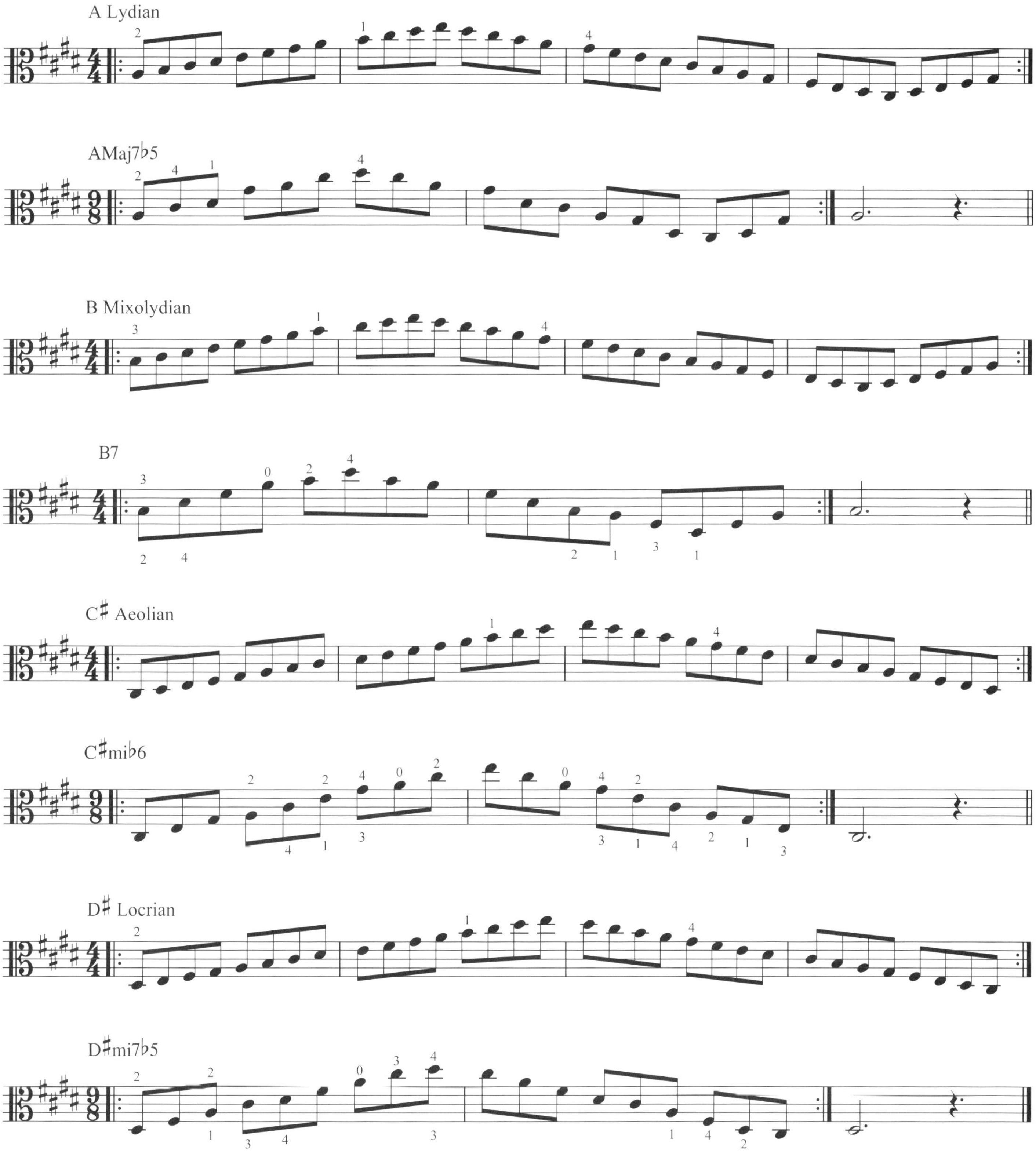

FIG. 5.10. Modes of E Major

Note that chords are expressed here with sharps that you'll see more commonly expressed with flats in lead sheets. For instance, you'll see E♭mi7♭5 more often than you'll see D♯mi7♭5. Make sure you learn to associate every scale and chord that you learn in a sharp key with its enharmonic equivalent in a flat key, and vice versa.

MODES OF A MAJOR

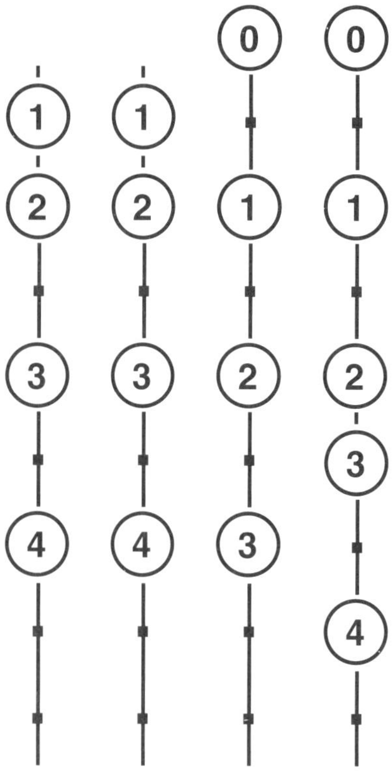

A Ionian

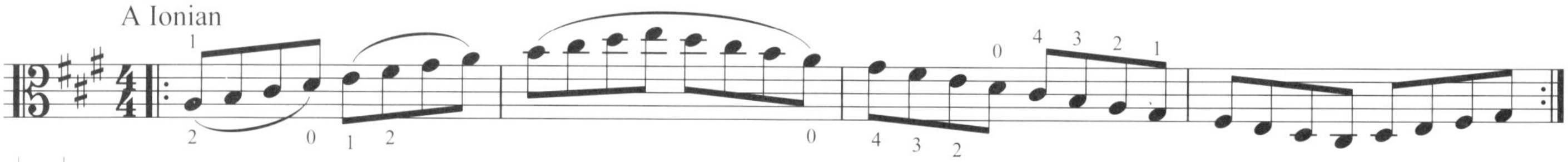

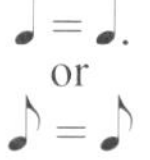

AMaj7

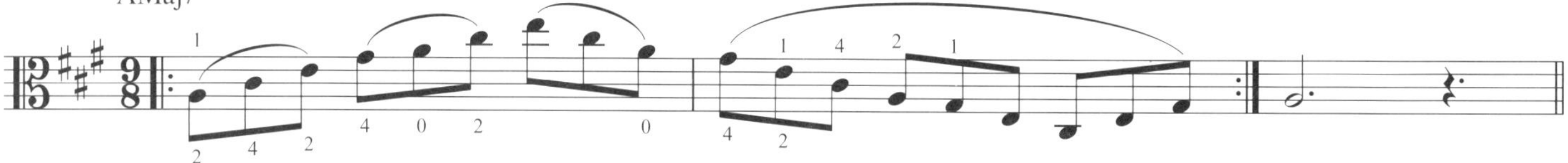

B Dorian

Fingerings Simile...

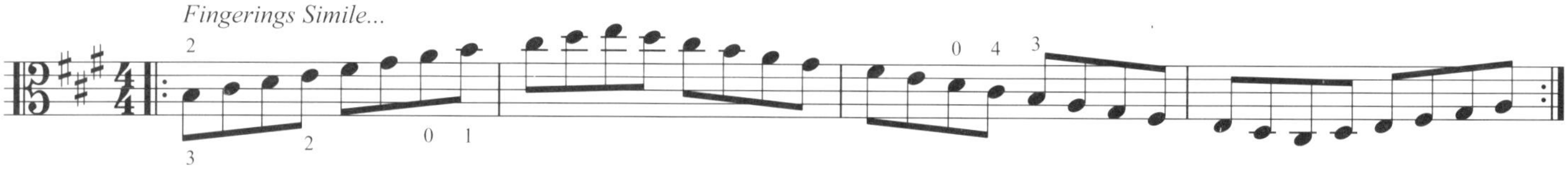

Bmi7

remain in first pos.

remain in half pos.

C♯ Phrygian

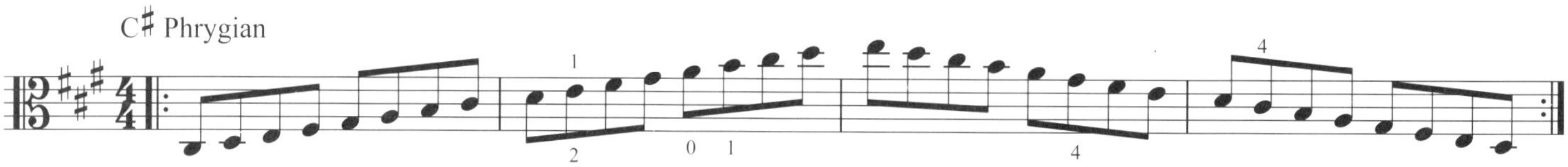

C♯sus(♭9)

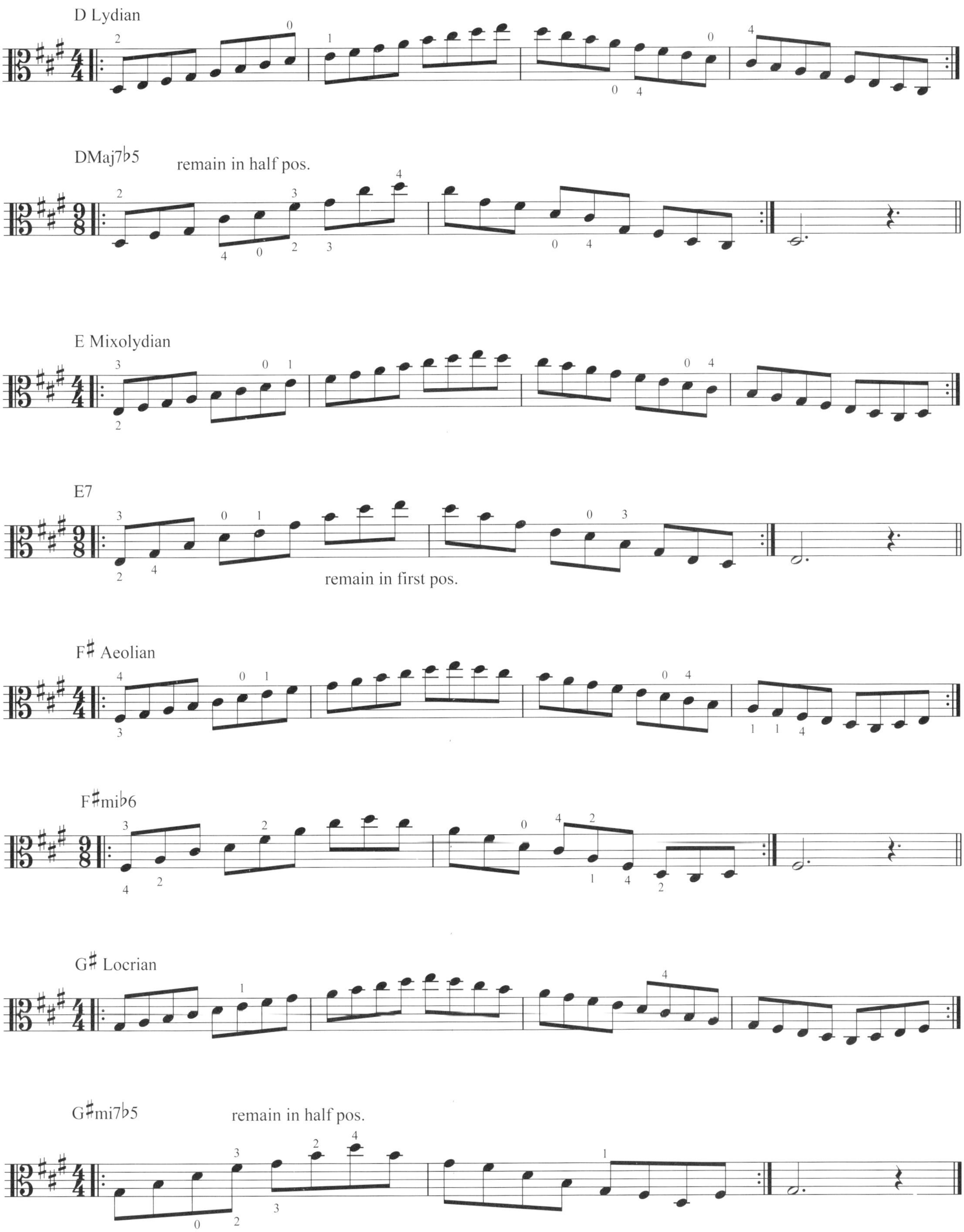

FIG. 5.11. Modes of A Major

MODES OF D MAJOR

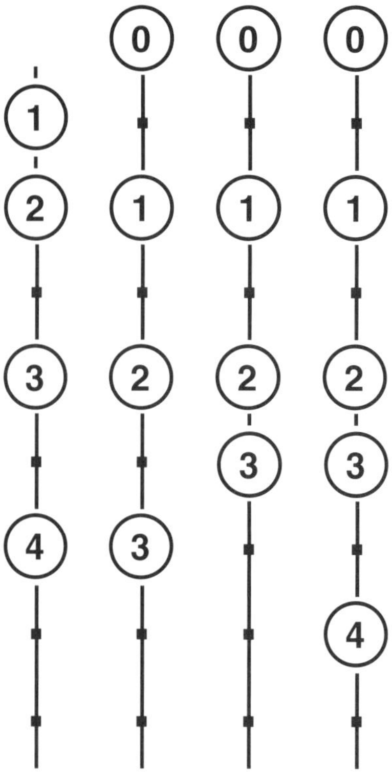

D Ionian

♩ = ♩.
or
♪ = ♪

DMaj7

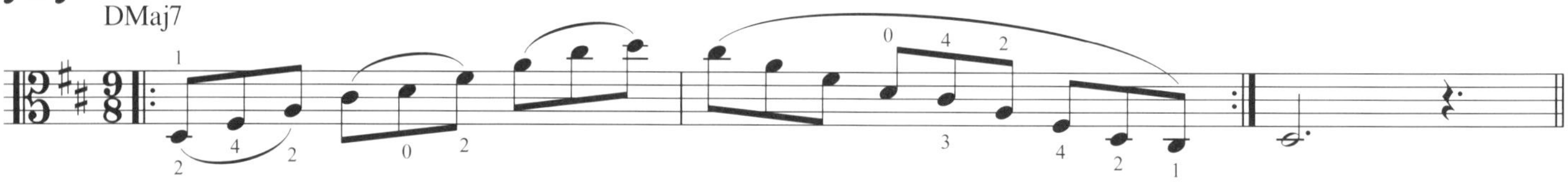

E Dorian

Emi7

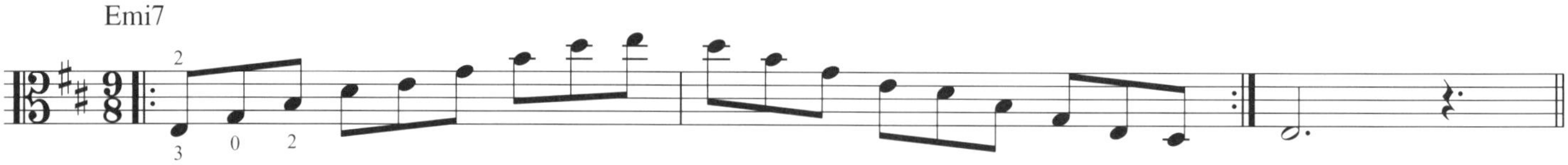

F♯ Phrygian

F♯sus(♭9)

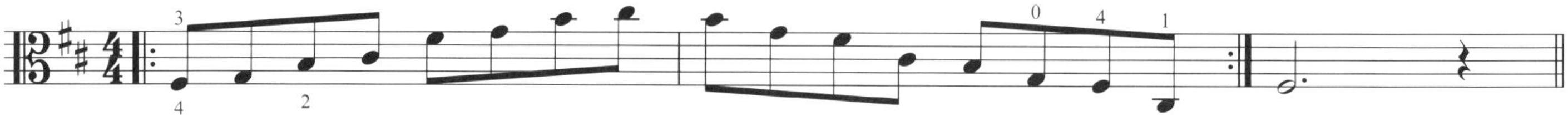

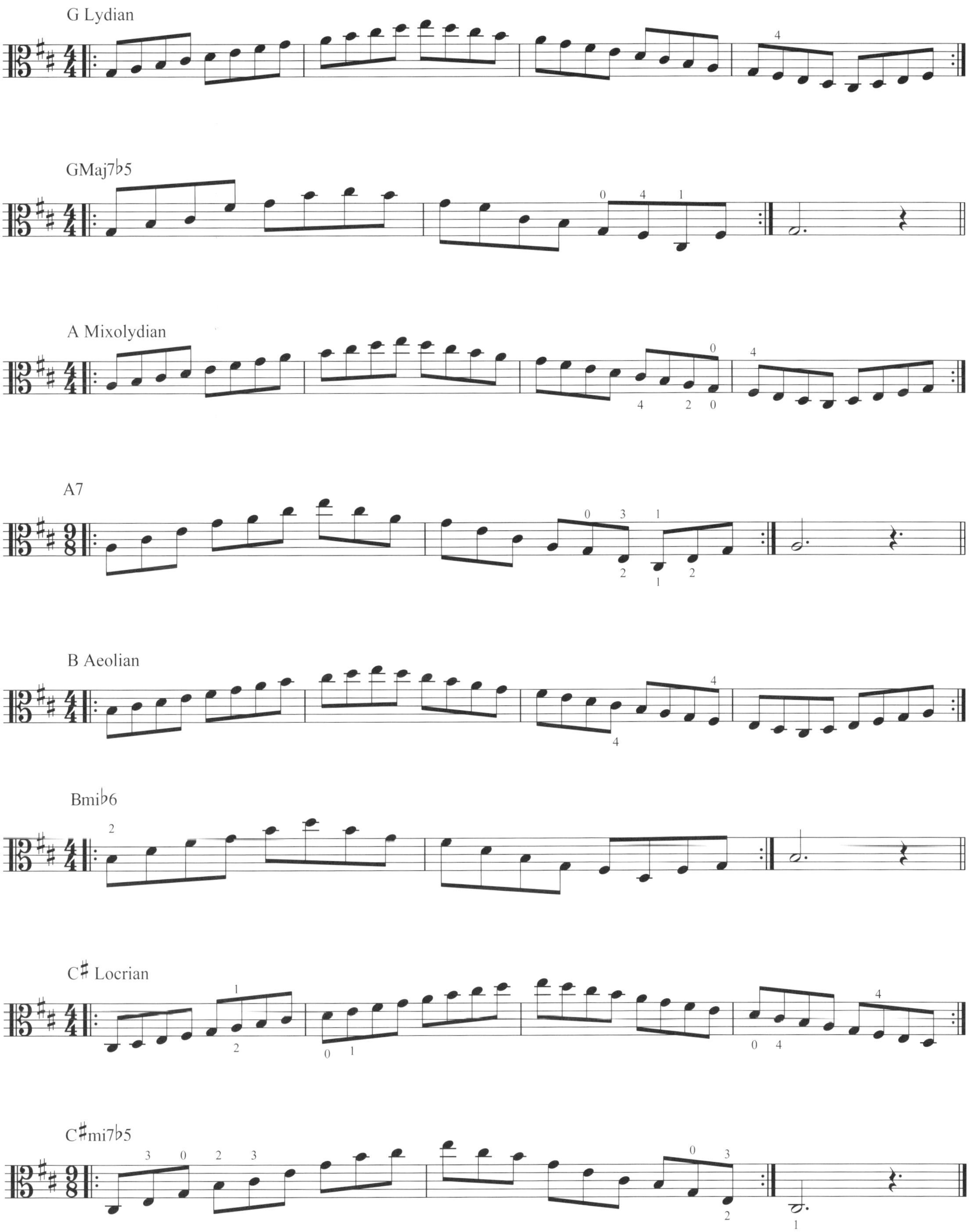

FIG. 5.12. Modes of D Major

CHAPTER 6

Modes on a Tonal Center

Now that you've practiced all seven modes in all twelve keys, let's play the modes from a single unchanging pitch. We'll call this the modes "on" C, instead of "in" C. The tonal center (C) remains constant, as accidentals create the intervallic structures (half-step placements) you saw in figure 4.1.

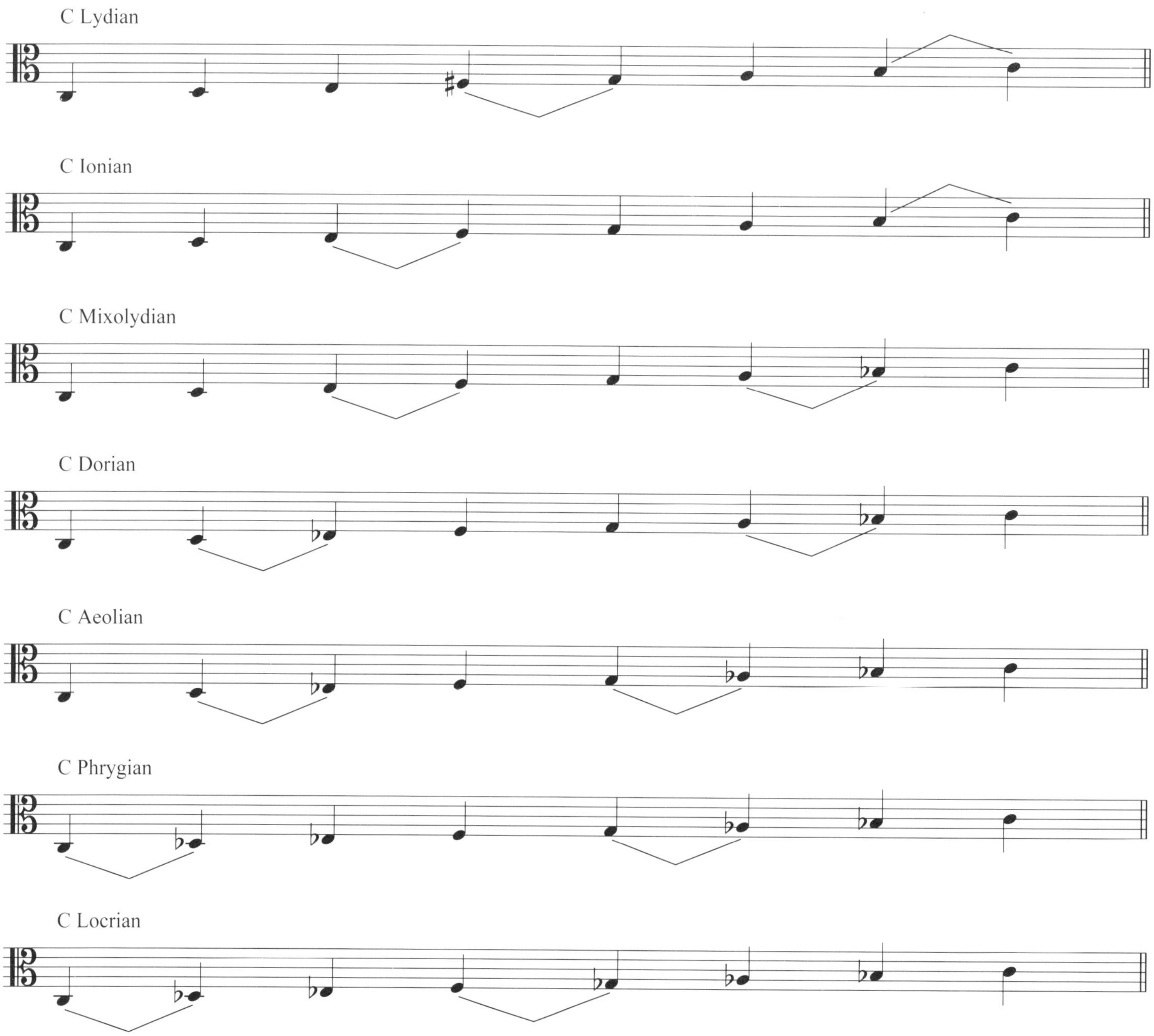

FIG. 6.1. The Seven Modes on C

When the seven modes are organized this way, something very interesting happens. Notice the way the half steps move to the left, one at a time, as you read down the page. Each successive scale is similar to the one that precedes it, except for one note, which is moved down a half step. In the second mode, F♯ has changed to F. Then B changes to B♭, E to E♭, etc. As these notes are lowered, we see the sharp deleted, then flats added in the order of flats. This means that the key signature is cycling around the circle of fifths! C Lydian consists of the same group of pitches as G major. C Mixolydian has one flat, like F major. C Dorian is the same pitch set as B♭ major, followed by E♭ (C Aeolian), A♭ (C Phrygian), and D♭ (C Locrian).

The acronym for this order of modes is more pronounceable than "IDPLMAL." It's sometimes referred to as "LIMDAPL" (pronounced "lim dapple"). In the pages that follow, the drill you played on the modes of the major keys is applied to the LIMDAPL modal order or "mode cycle."

Here are the modal exercises in the LIMDAPL order; I refer to them as the "LIMDAPL Exercises" with my students. Now you will play the seven modes on each of twelve tonal centers. Practicing the modes of a major scale in succession (especially without the associated arpeggios) doesn't provide much contrast between modes. They can all begin to sound like the major scale from which they are derived. Practicing the seven modes in this order, starting each one on the same pitch, provides much more contrast and color, as you will hear.

LIMDAPL ON C

Lydian

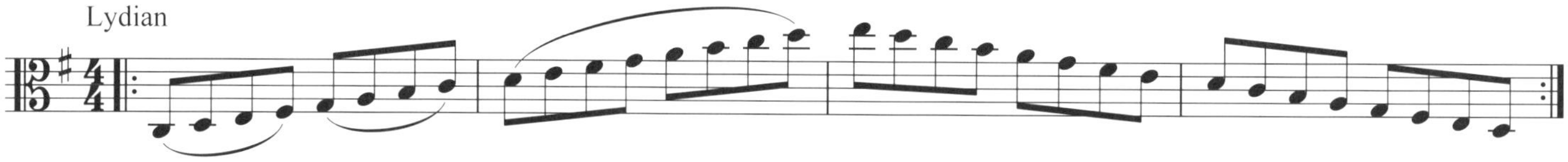

Maj7♭5

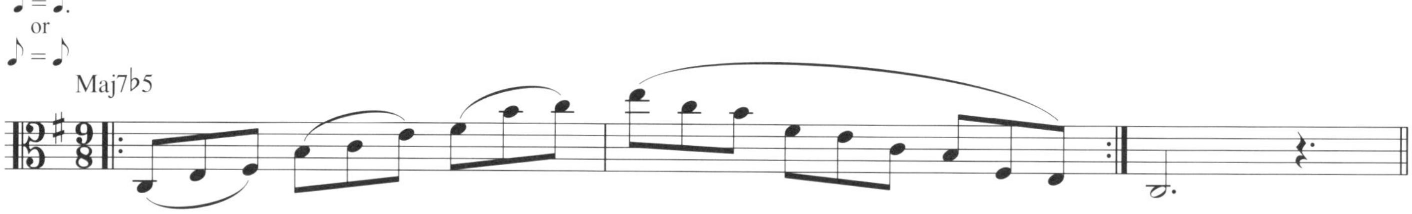

Ionian

Maj7

Mixolydian

7

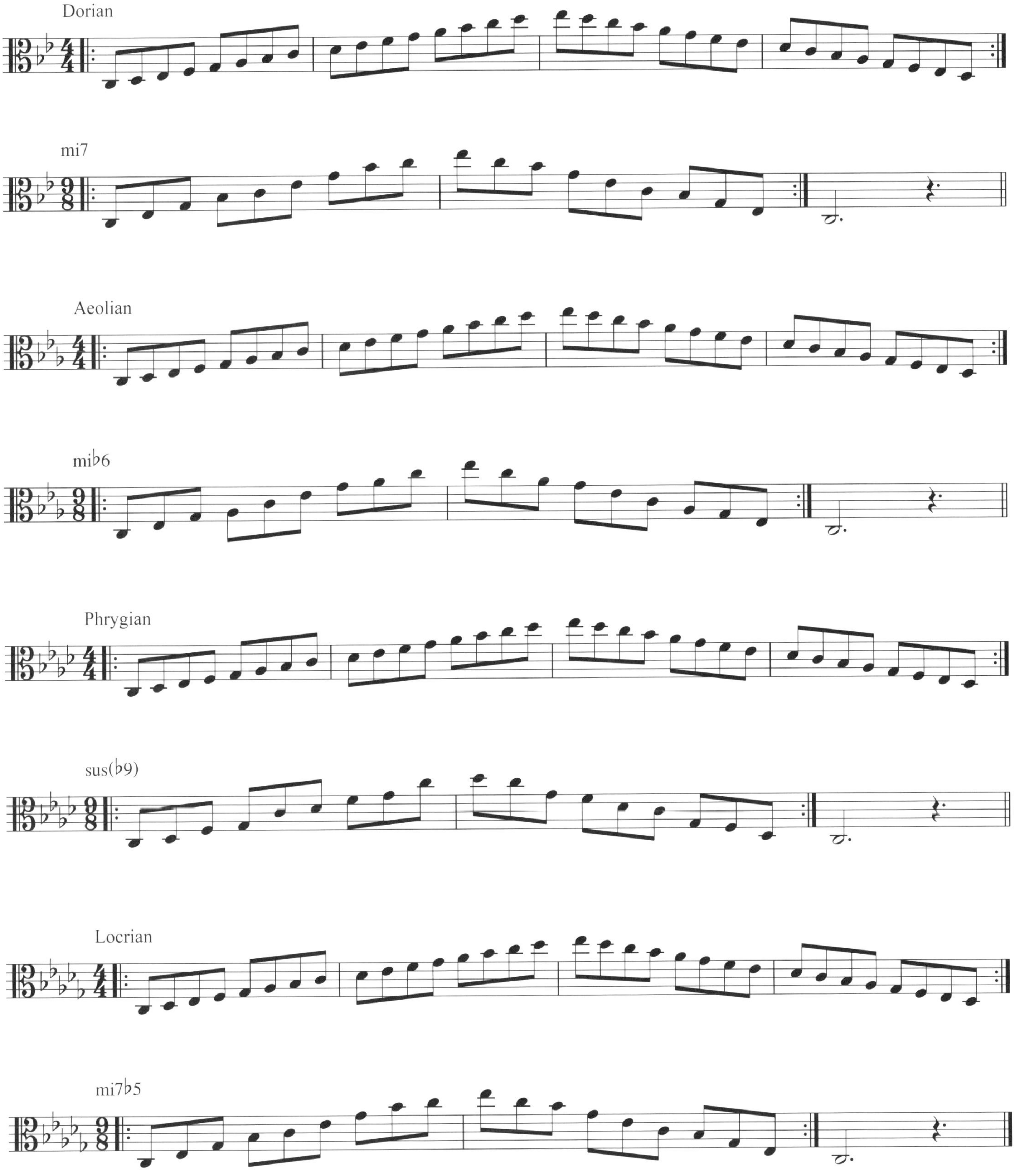

FIG. 6.2. LIMDAPL on C

LIMDAPL ON F

Lydian

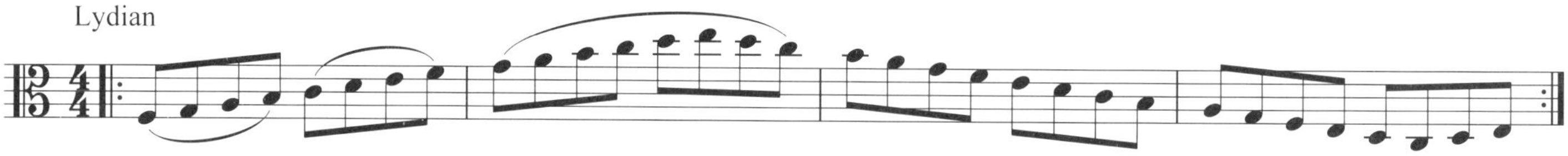

Maj7♭5

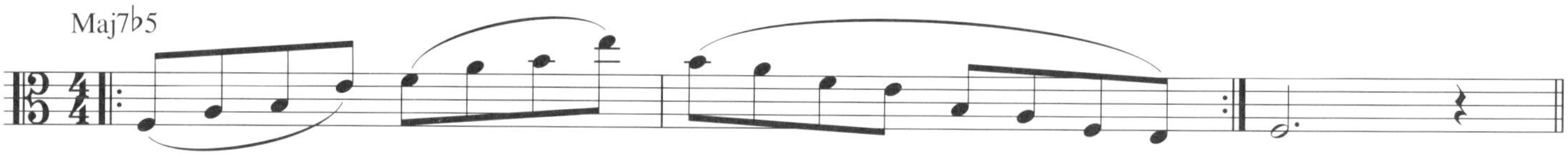

Ionian

♩ = ♩.
or
♪ = ♪

Maj7

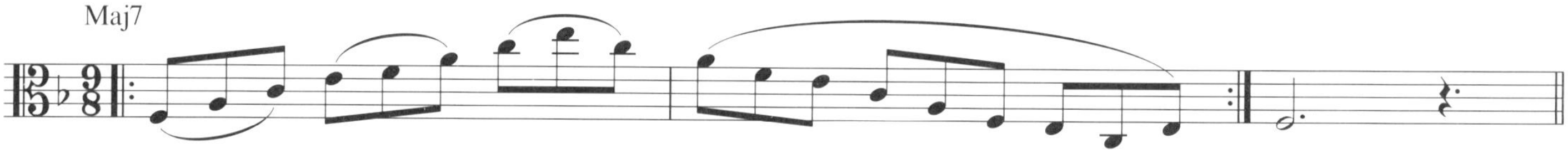

Mixolydian

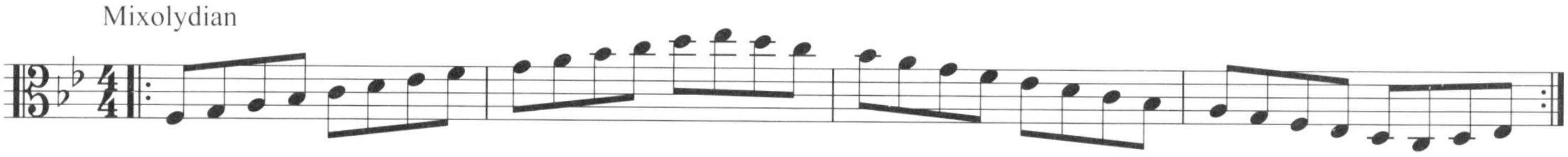

7

Dorian

mi7

Aeolian

mi♭6

Phrygian

sus(♭9)

Locrian

mi7♭5

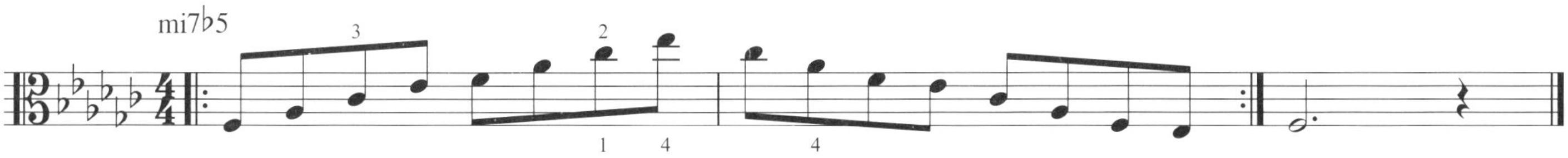

FIG. 6.3. LIMDAPL on F

LIMDAPL ON B♭

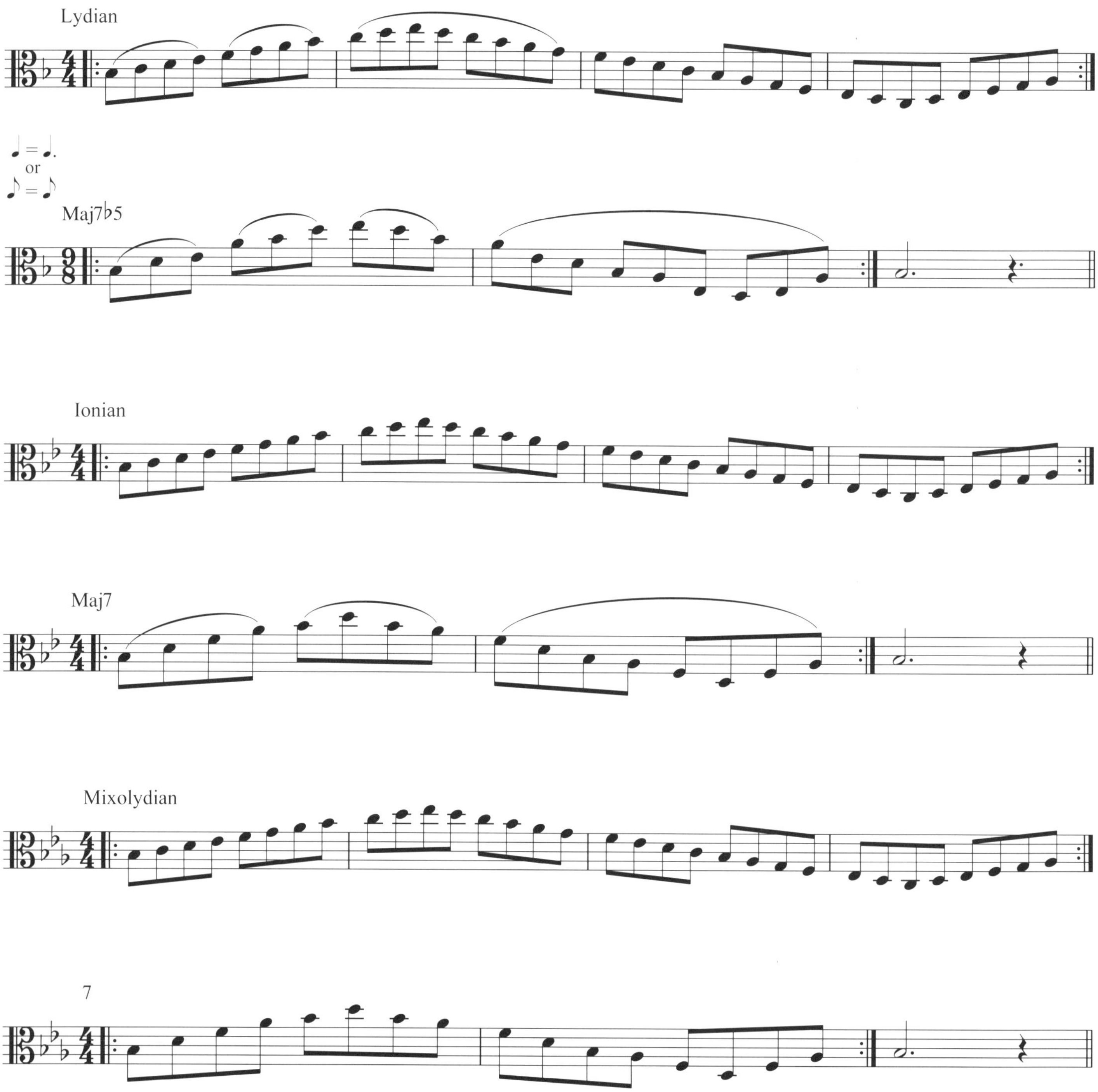

Dorian

mi7

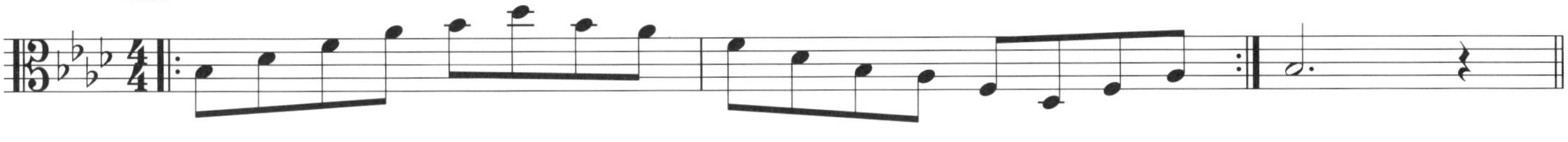

Aeolian

mi♭6

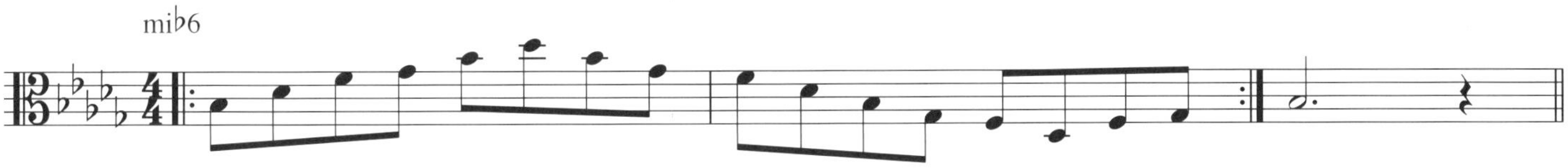

Phrygian

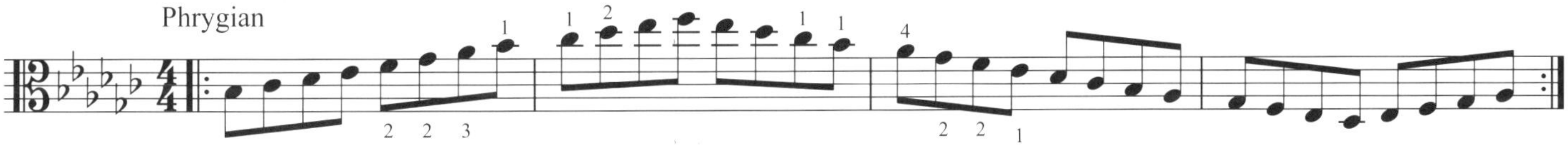

sus(♭9)

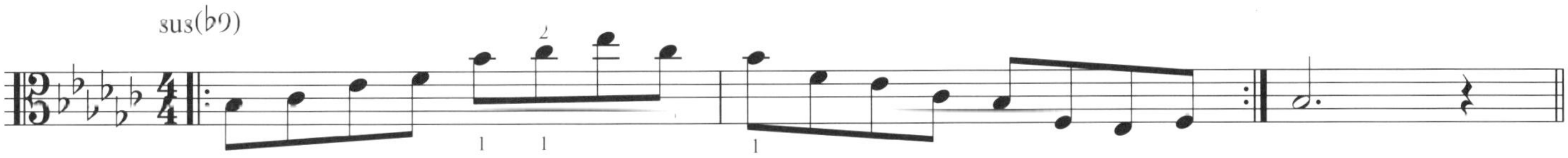

Locrian

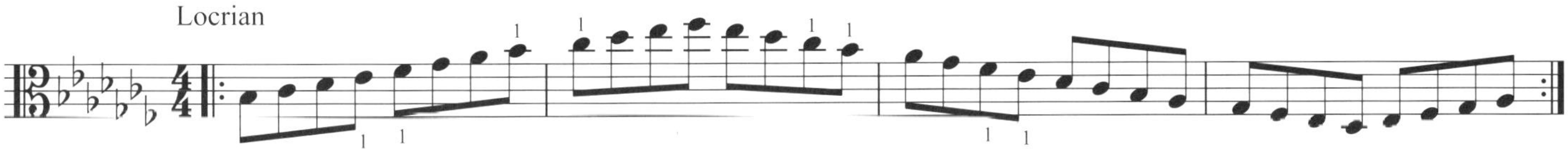

mi7♭5

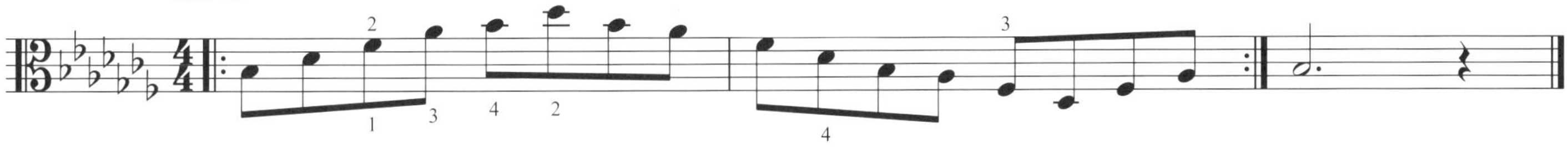

FIG. 6.4. LIMDAPL on B♭

LIMDAPL ON E♭/D♯

For pitches with enharmonic equivalents (e.g., E♭ and D♯), you will notice a change during the routine. The equivalent pitch name is used, and the key signature changes from six flats to five sharps. It is arguably easier to read that way, and heads off the need for double flats, going forward.

Lydian

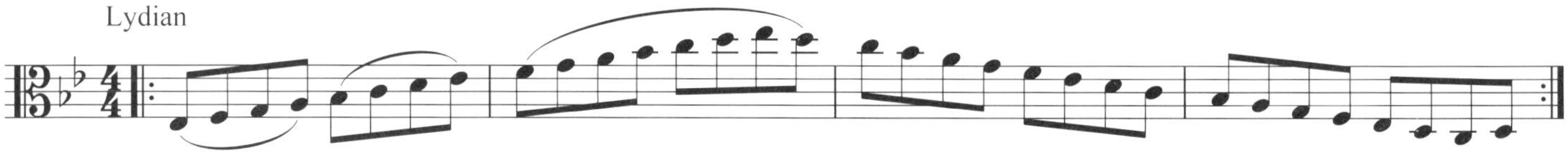

♩ = ♩.
or
♪ = ♪

Maj7♭5

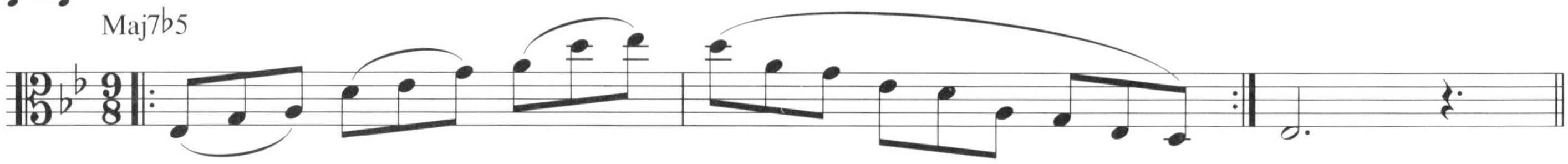

Ionian

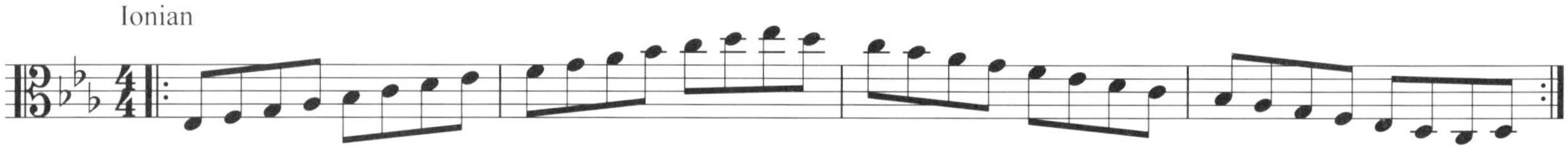

Maj7

Mixolydian

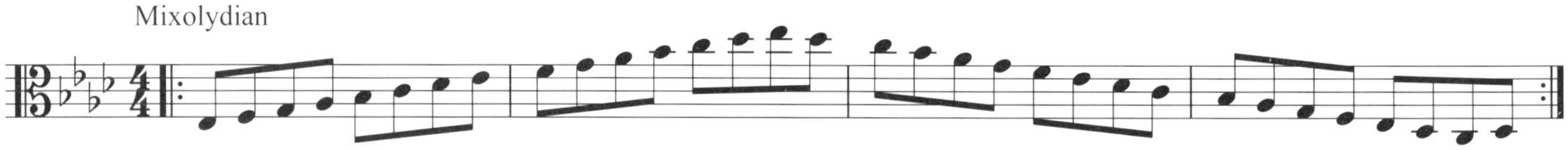

7

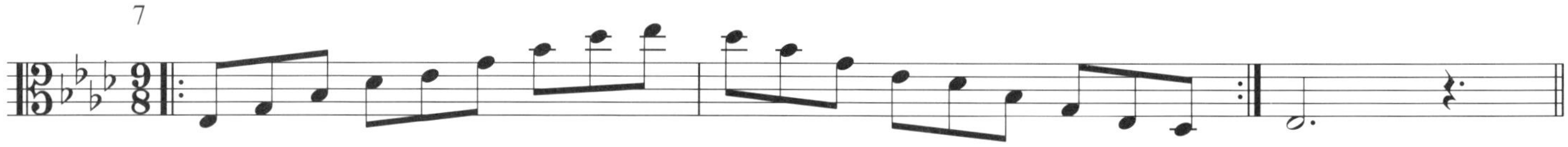

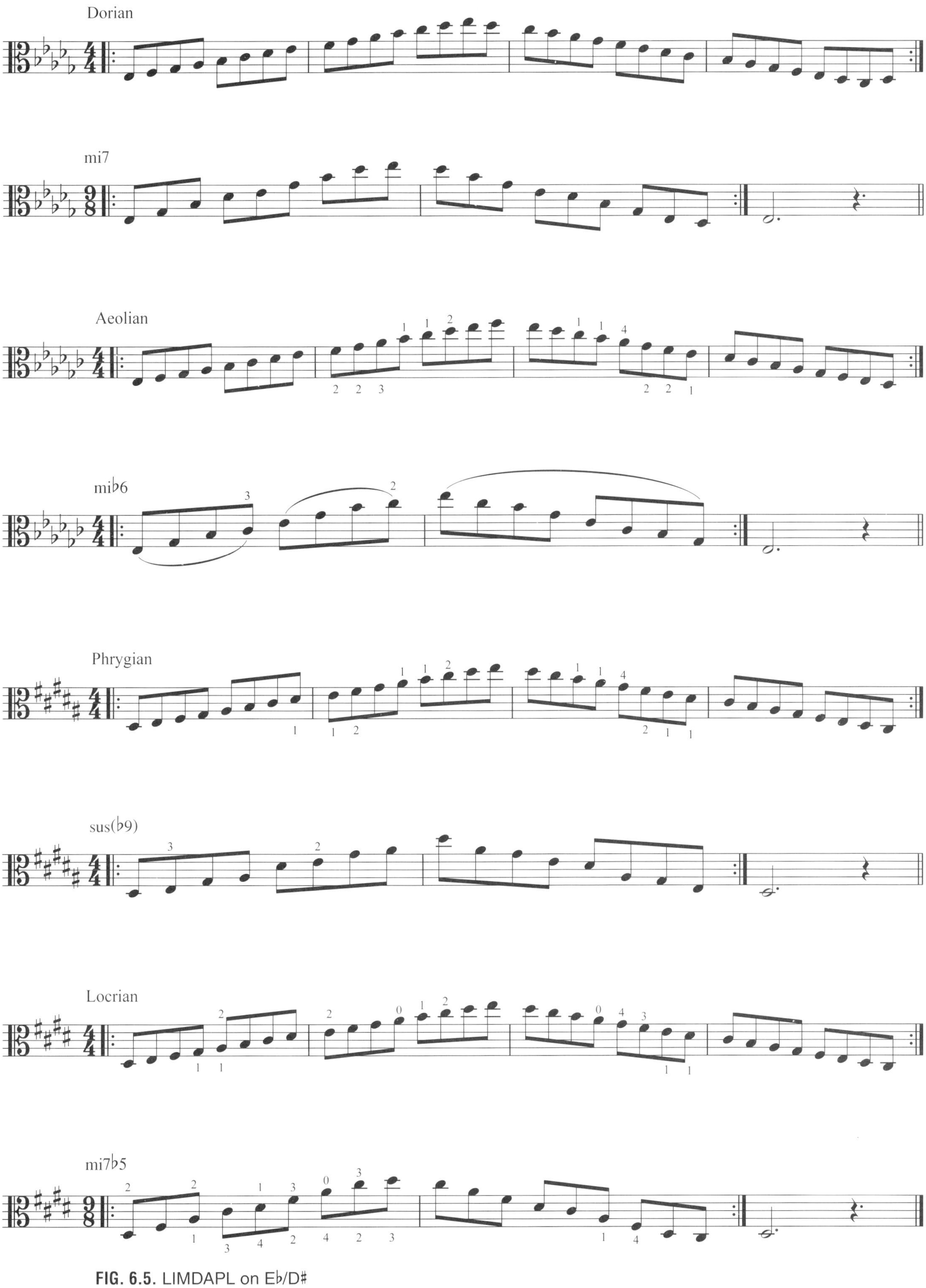

FIG. 6.5. LIMDAPL on E♭/D♯

LIMDAPL ON A♭/G♯

Lydian

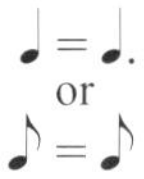

Maj7♭5

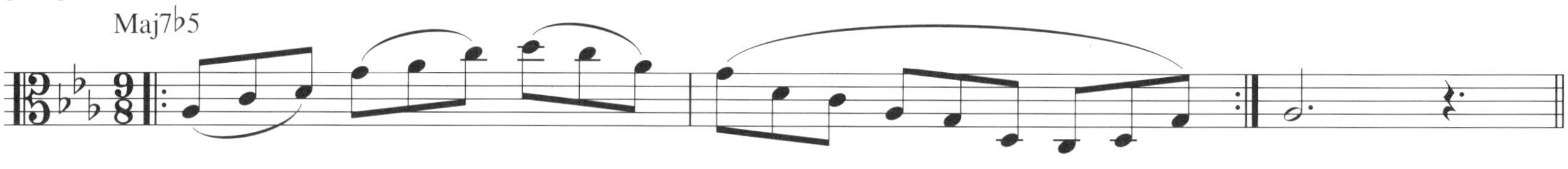

Ionian

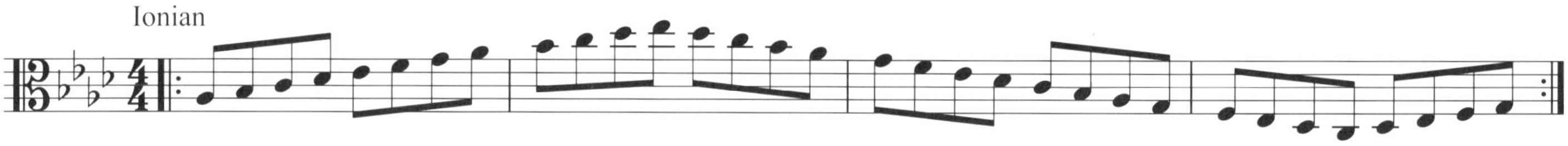

Maj7

Mixolydian

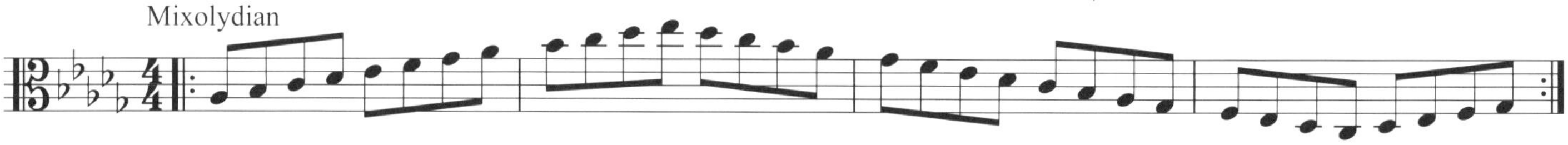

7

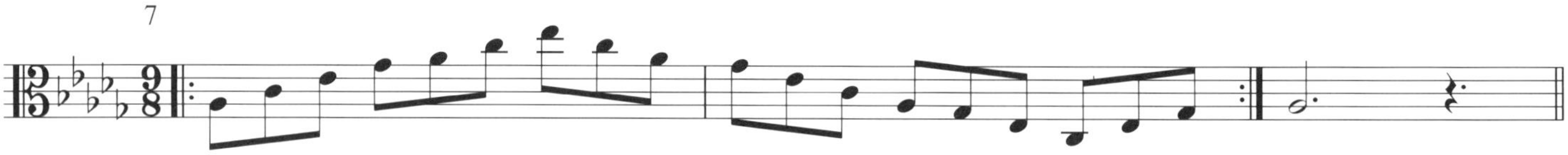

FIG. 6.6. LIMDAPL on A♭/G♯

LIMDAPL ON D♭/C♯

Lydian

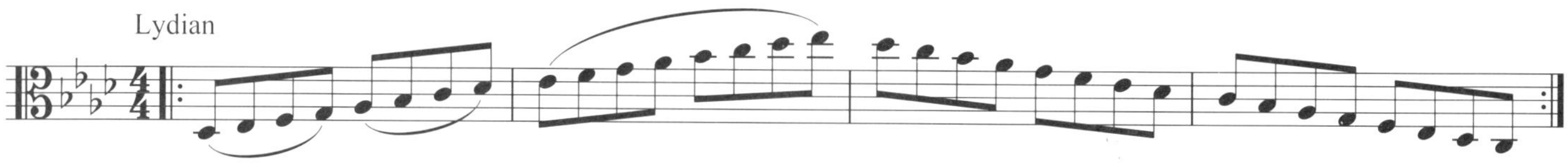

Maj7♭5

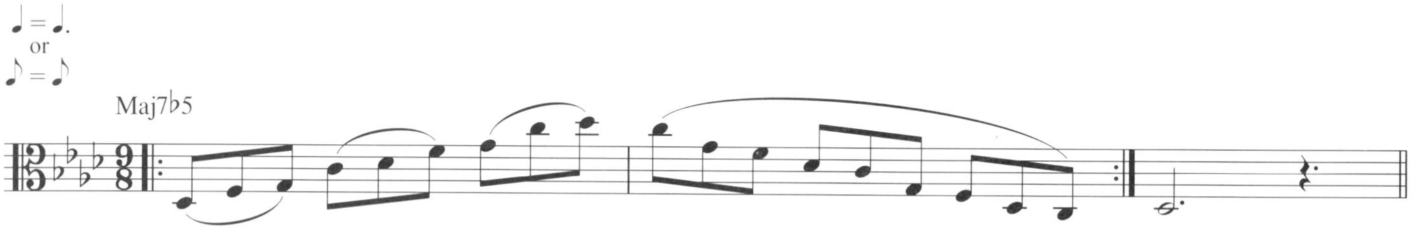

Ionian

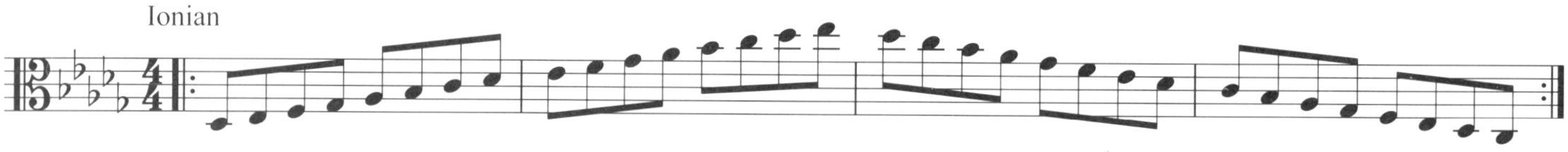

Maj7

Mixolydian

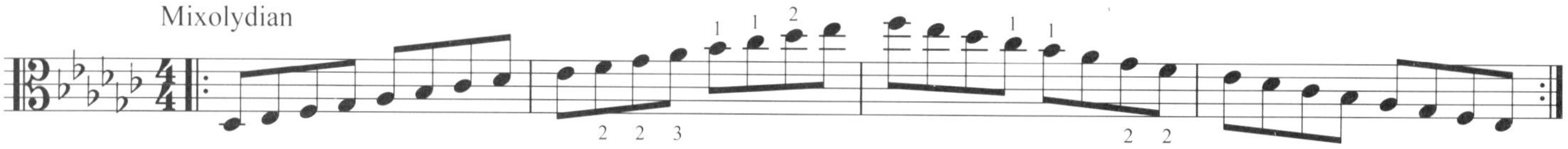

7

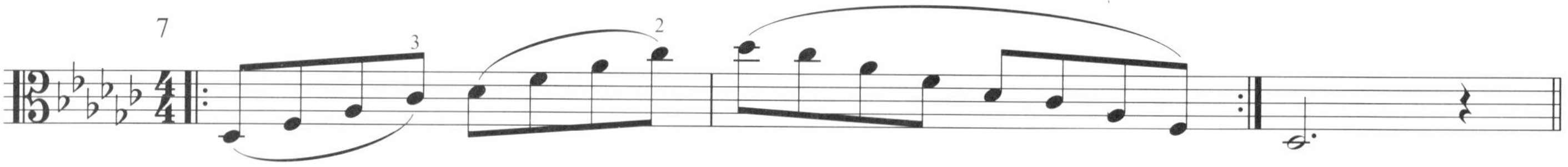

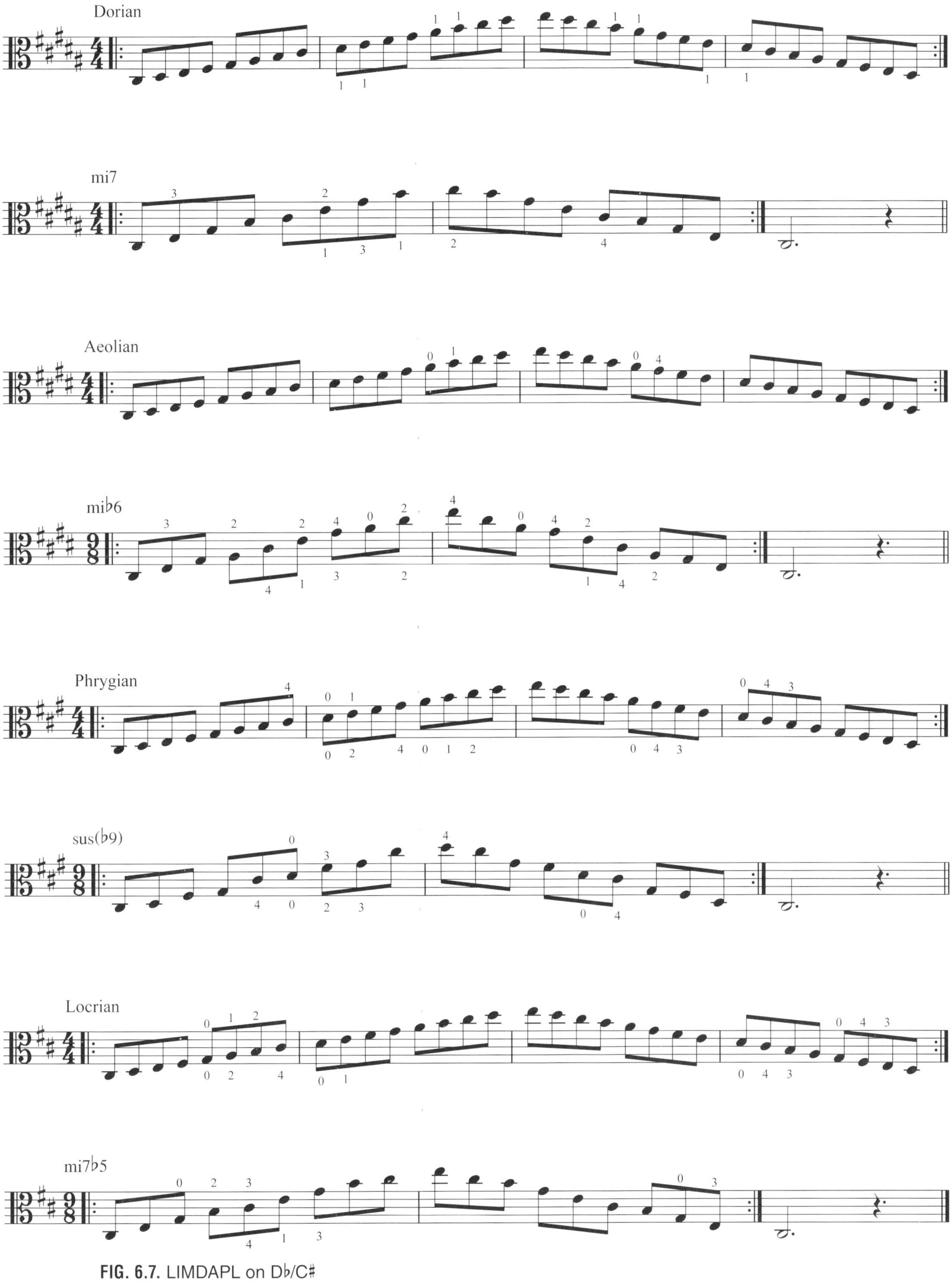

FIG. 6.7. LIMDAPL on D♭/C♯

LIMDAPL ON G♭/F♯

Lydian

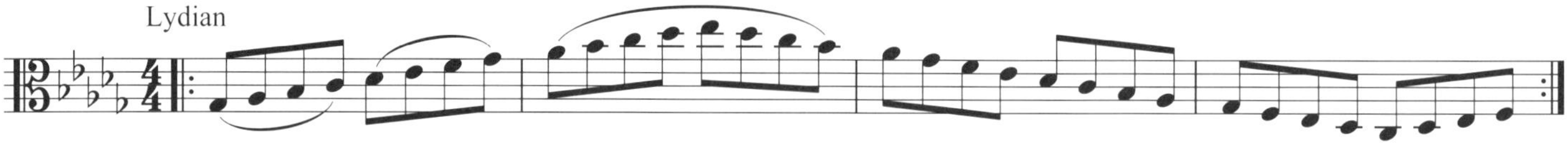

Maj7♭5

Ionian

Maj7

Mixolydian

7

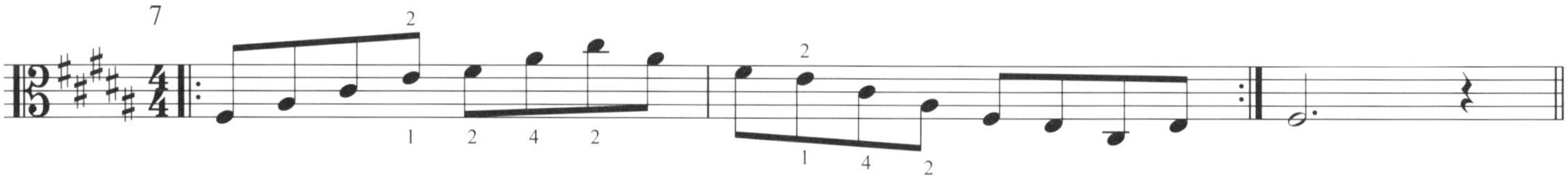

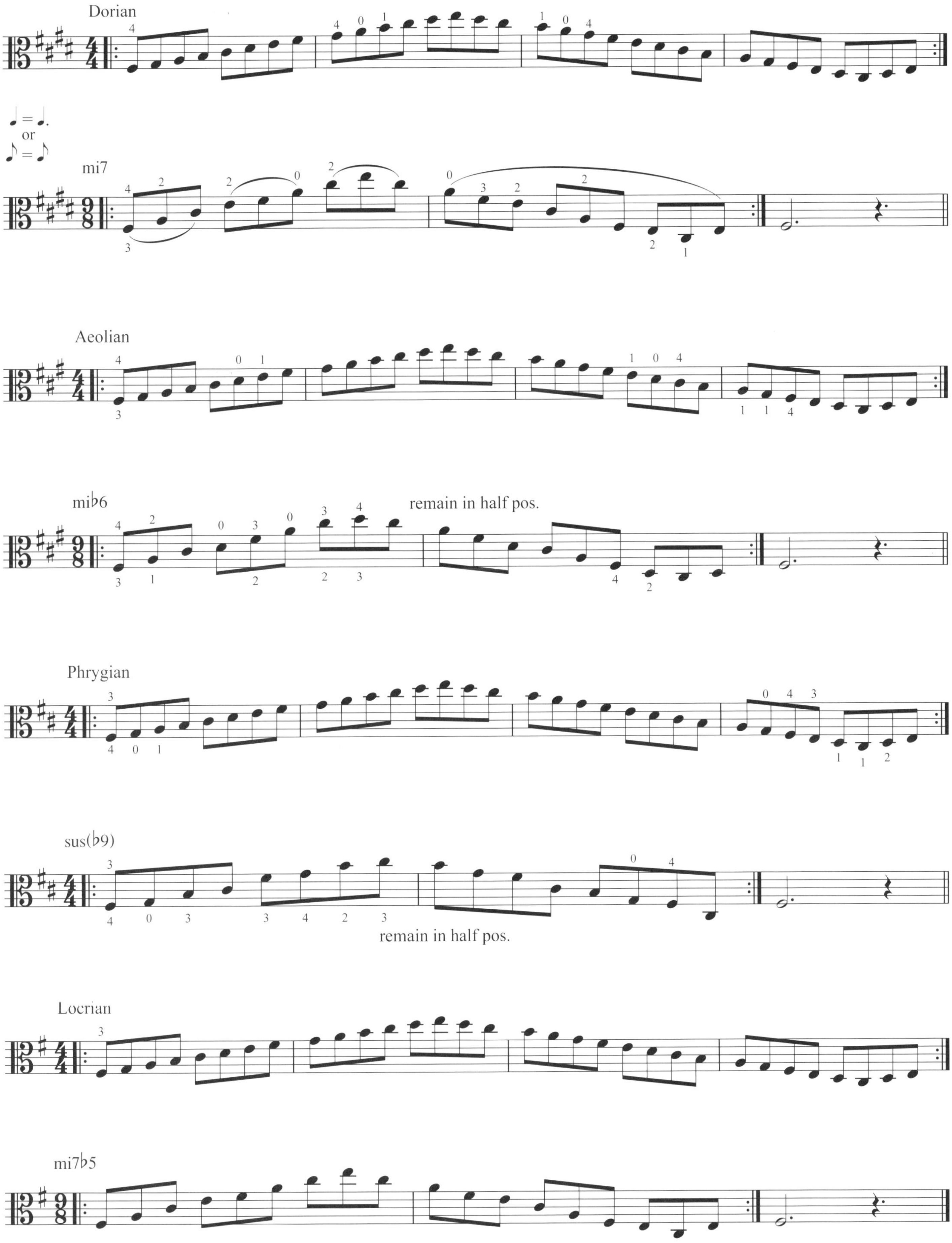

FIG. 6.8. LIMDAPL on G♭/F♯

LIMDAPL ON B

Lydian

Maj7♭5

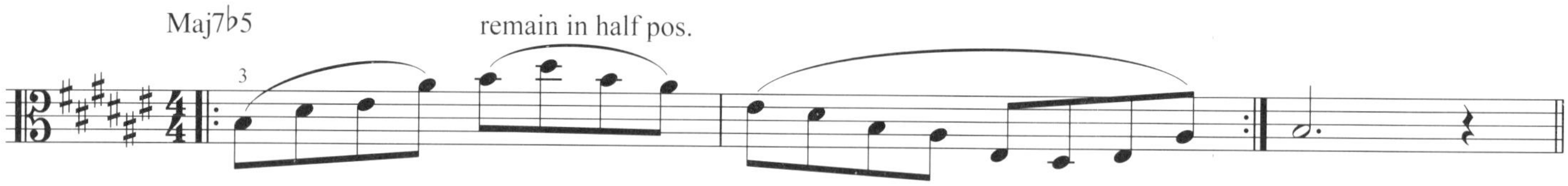

Ionian

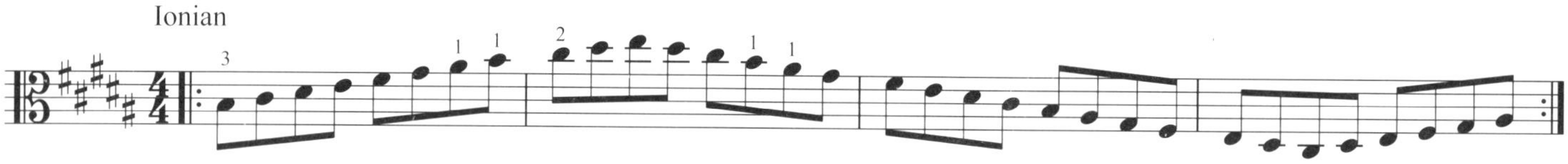

Maj7

Mixolydian

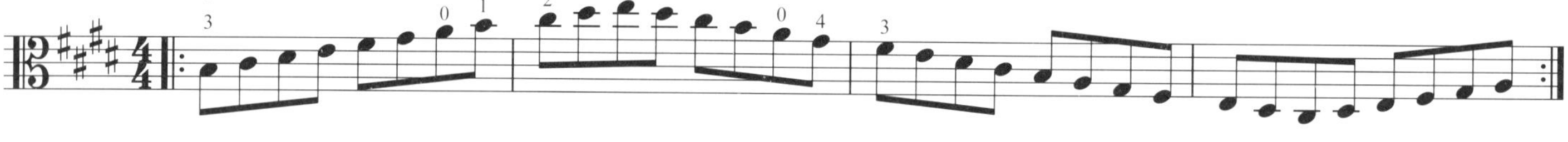

7

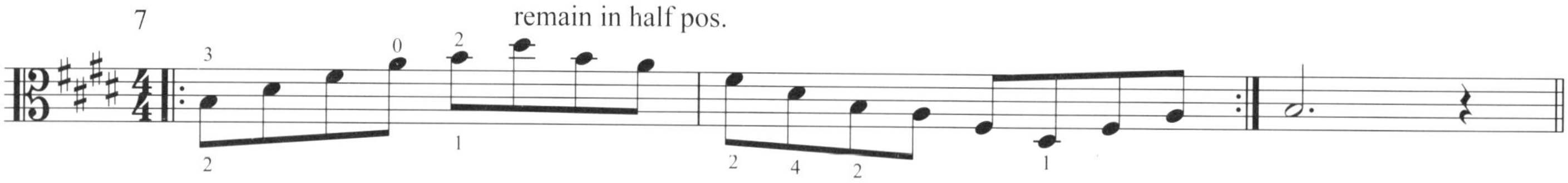

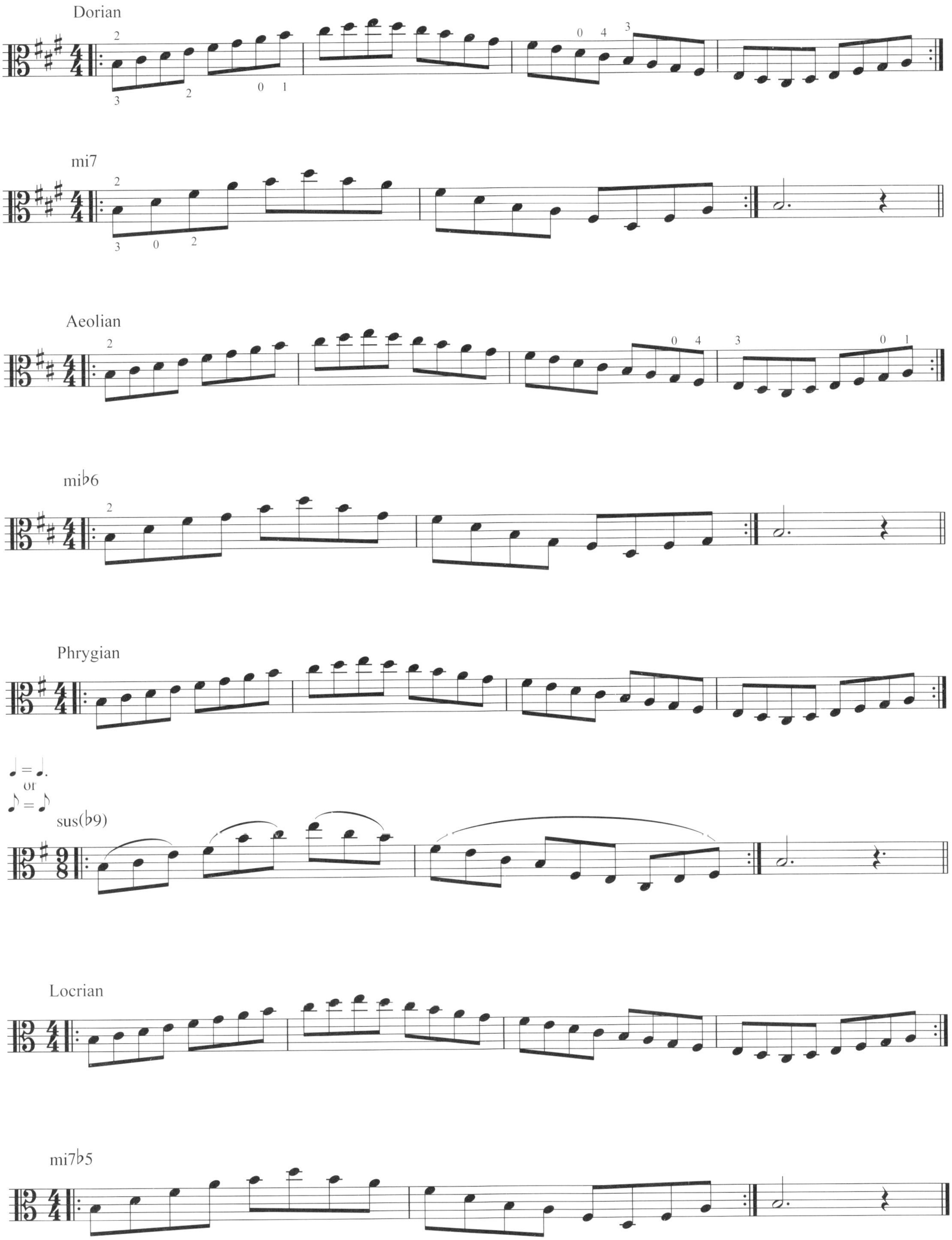

FIG. 6.9. LIMDAPL on B

LIMDAPL ON E

Lydian

Maj7♭5

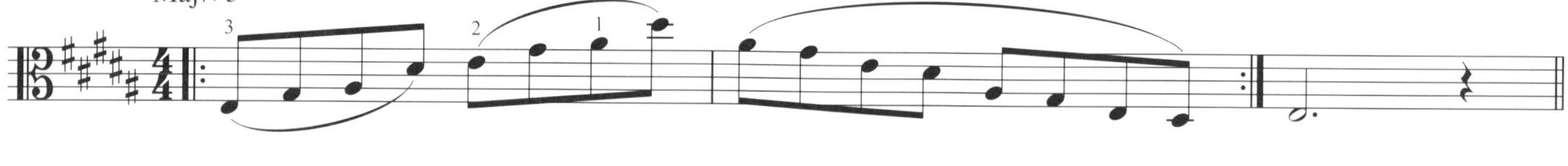

Ionian

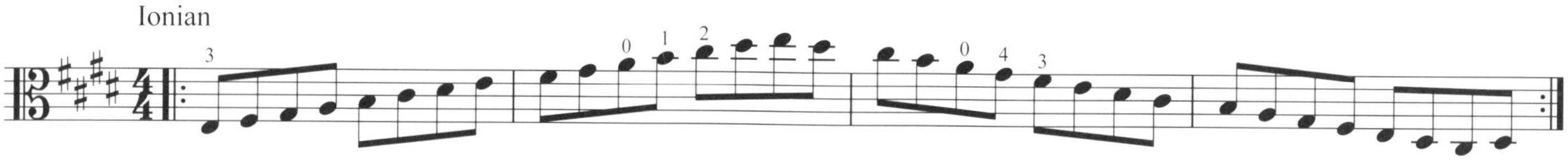

Maj7

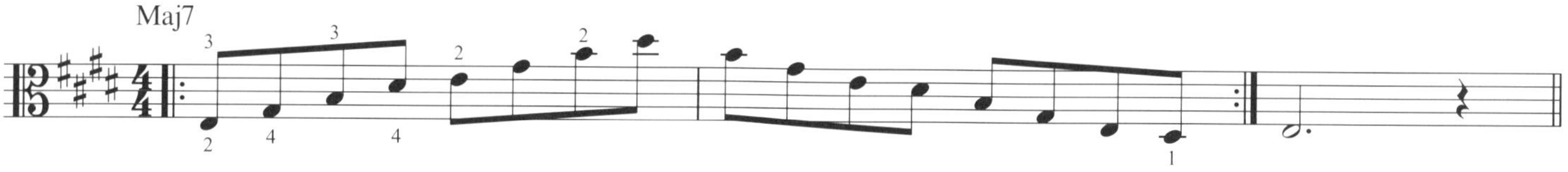

Mixolydian

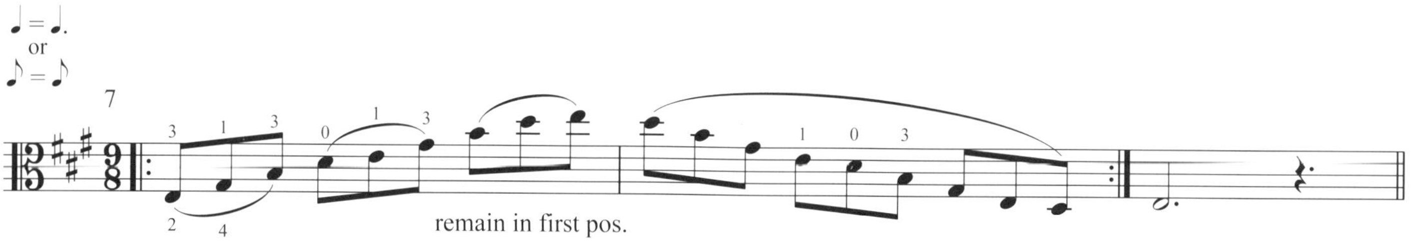

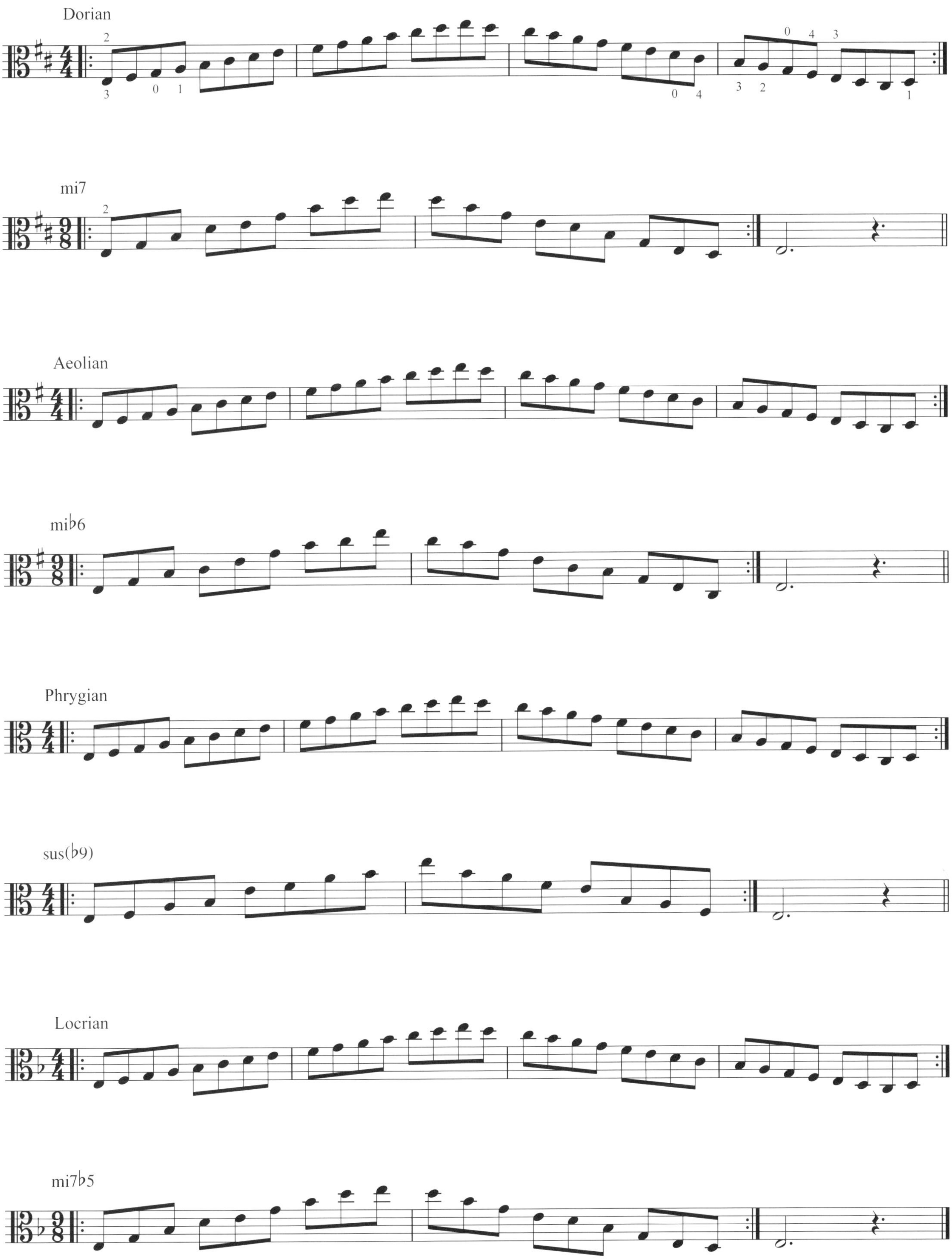

FIG. 6.10. LIMDAPL on E

LIMDAPL ON A

Lydian

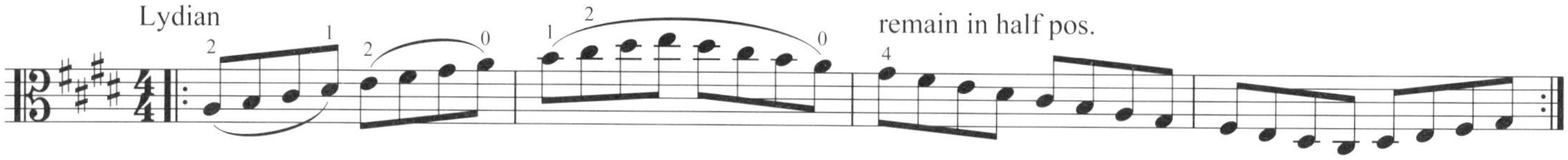

♩ = ♩.
or
♪ = ♪

Maj7♭5

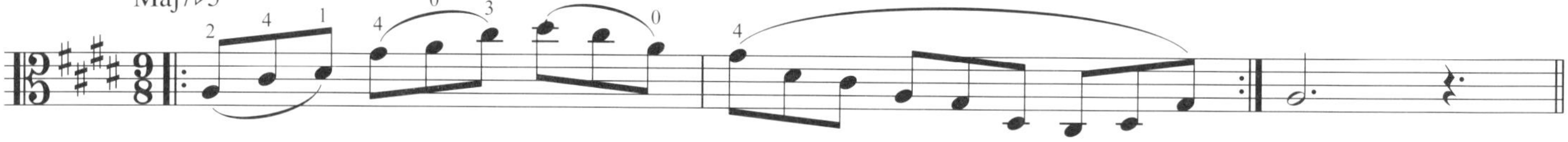

Ionian

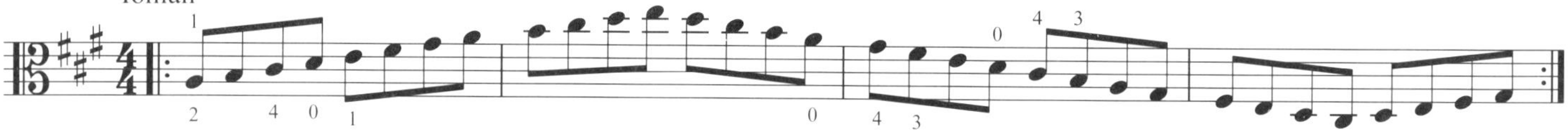

Maj7

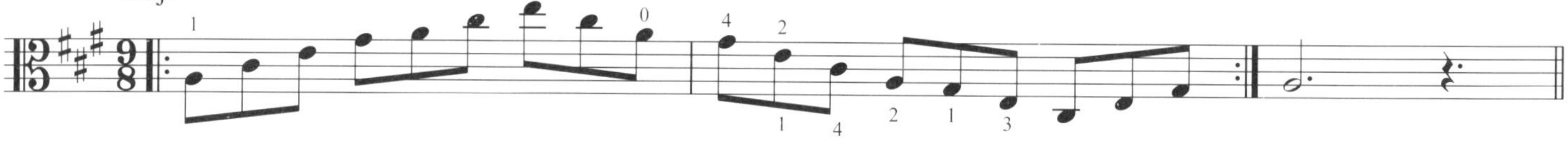

Mixolydian

7

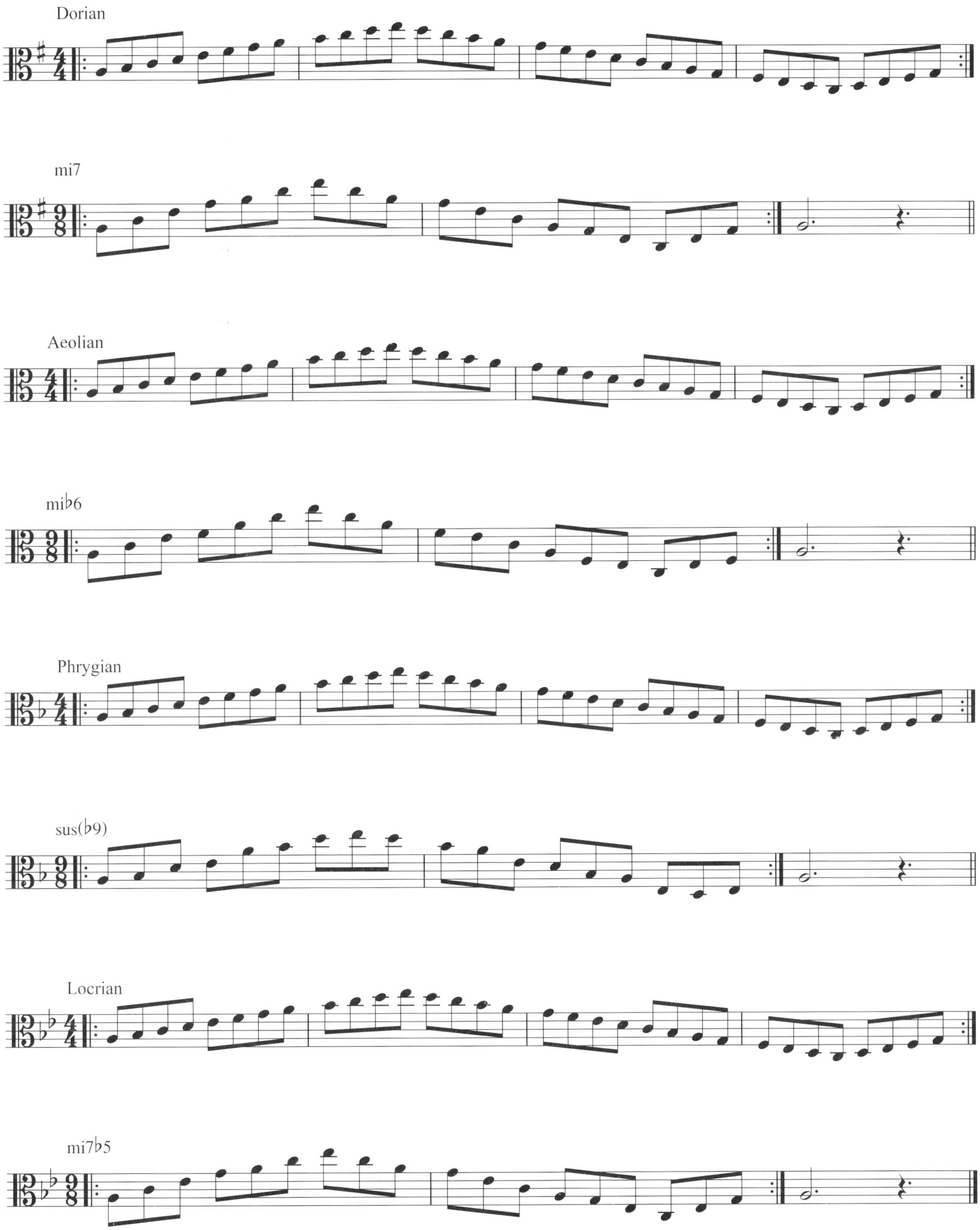

FIG. 6.11. LIMDAPL on A

LIMDAPL ON D

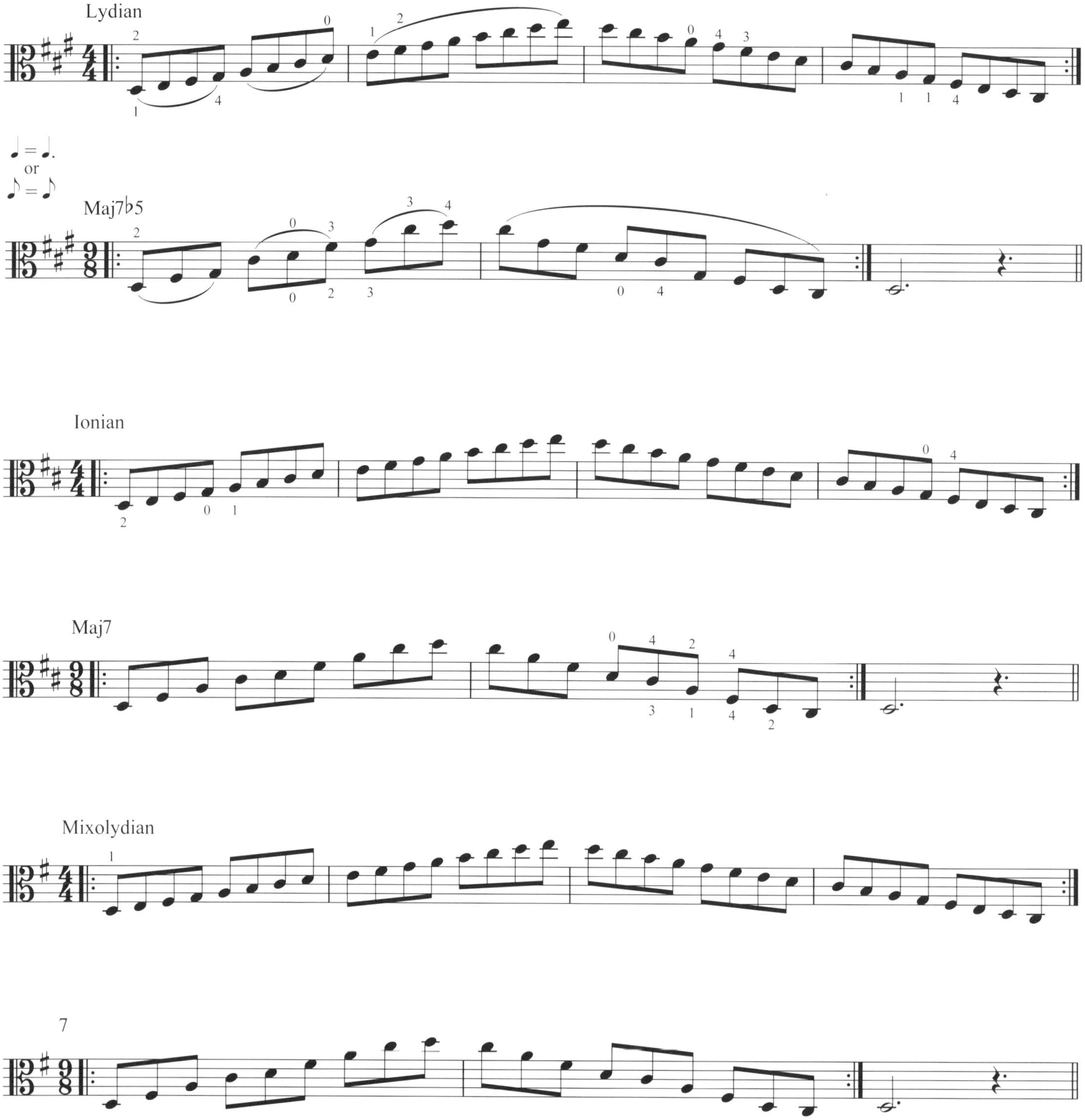

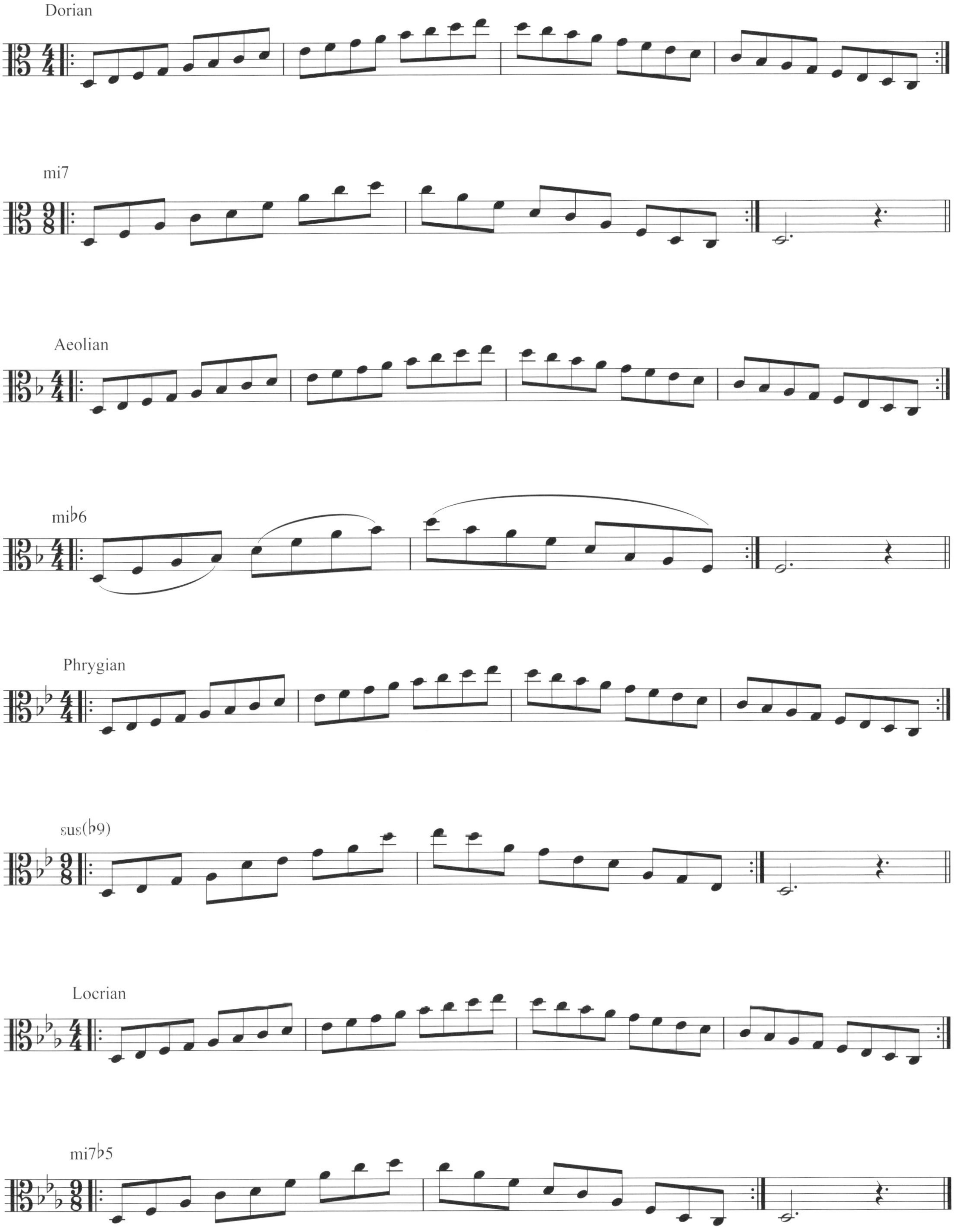

FIG. 6.12. LIMDAPL on D

LIMDAPL ON G

Lydian

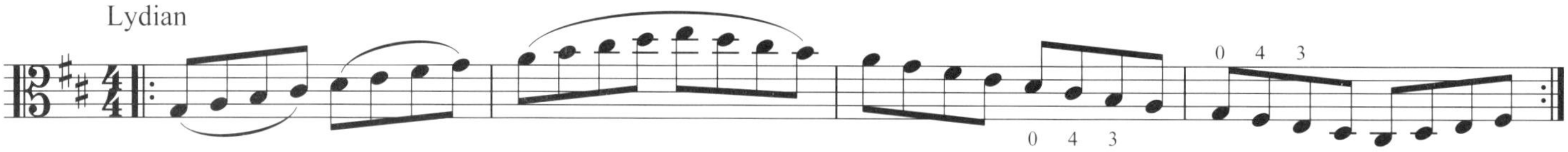

Maj7♭5

Ionian

Maj7

Mixolydian

7

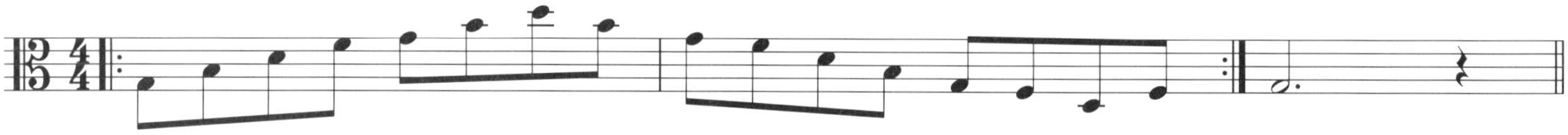

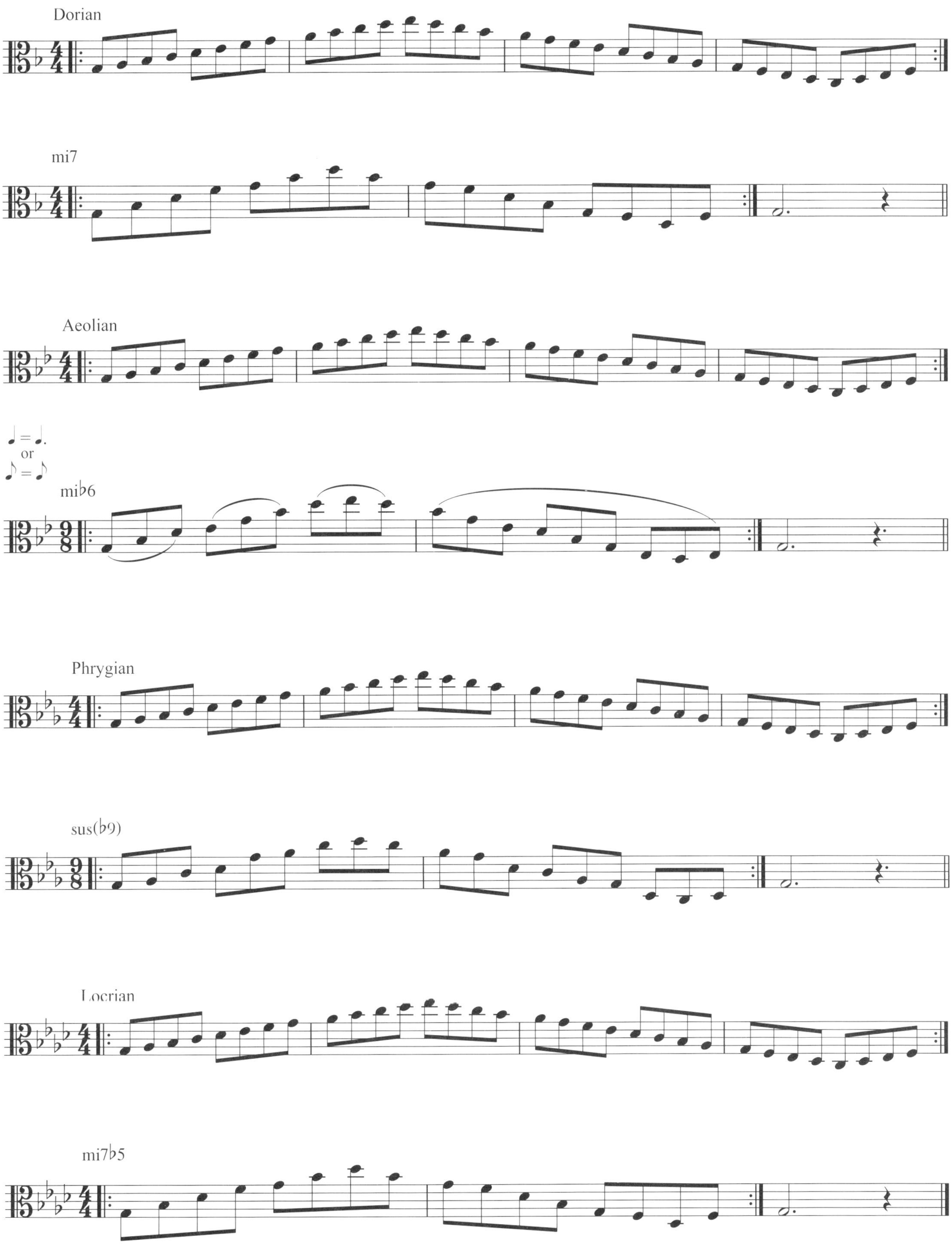

FIG. 6.13. LIMDAPL on G

CHAPTER 7

Using Play-Along Accompaniment

Now, you'll want to put the scales and arpeggios practiced in chapters 5 and 6 to work as source material for improvisation. To do that, you'll need to hear some chords. You can use the audio files provided at the Hal Leonard website. Log in with the code provided on the first page of this book. You will find a link to an audio file for each key that plays the chord progression for the "modes in a key" exercises in chapter 5 (figure 7.1). You will also find twelve links for the LIMDAPL chord progression. In both progressions, each chord is played for sixteen bars (figure 7.2). If you want to practice with one chord at a time, there are files for that, too. Before you tackle music with chords that change frequently, it's useful to learn to improvise on them one at a time.

Practice improvising over each chord progression using the notes of the indicated modes. Each chord region lasts for sixteen bars.

- "Modes in a Key" tracks include an audio file based on each key.
- "Modes on a Tonal Center" tracks include an audio file for each pitch, with all seven chords built from the same note.
- "Single-Chord Vamps" let you practice on one chord at a time.

Measures	Modes in a Key (IDPLMAL)		Modes on a Tonal Center (LIMDAPL)	
	Chord	Mode	Chord	Mode
1st 16 bars	Maj7 on root	Ionian	Maj7♭5	Lydian
2nd 16 bars	mi7 on 2nd degree	Dorian	Maj7	Ionian
3rd 16 bars	sus(♭9) on 3rd degree	Phrygian	7	Mixolydian
4th 16 bars	Maj7♭5 on 4th degree	Lydian	mi7	Dorian
5th 16 bars	7 on 5th degree	Mixolydian	mi♭6	Aeolian
6th 16 bars	mi♭6 on 6th degree	Aeolian	sus(♭9)	Phrygian
7th 16 bars	mi7♭5 on 7th degree	Locrian	mi7♭5	Locrian

FIG. 7.1. Reference for Sixteen-Bar Play-Along Progressions

MODES IN A KEY CHORD PROGRESSION

The roots of these chords are the scale degrees, in succession, of the key you've chosen. If you are in B♭, the chords are B♭Maj7, Cmi7, Dsus(♭9), E♭Maj7♭5, F7, etc.

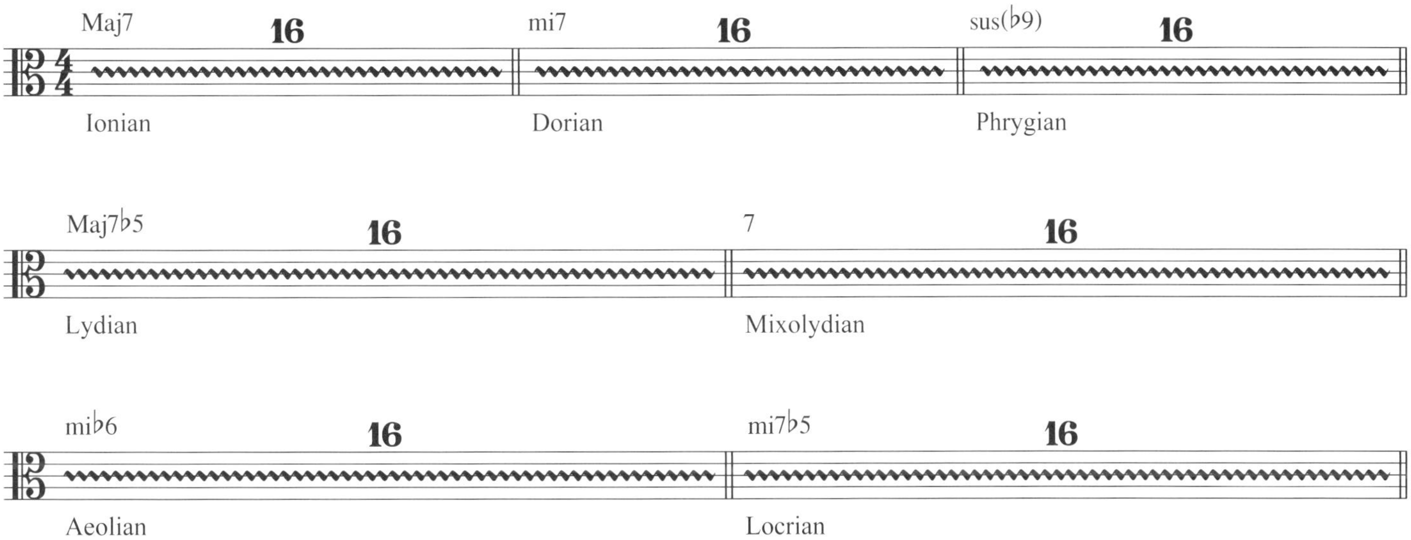

FIG. 7.2. Modes in a Key Chord Progression

MODES ON A TONAL CENTER CHORD PROGRESSION

All seven of these chords have the same root.

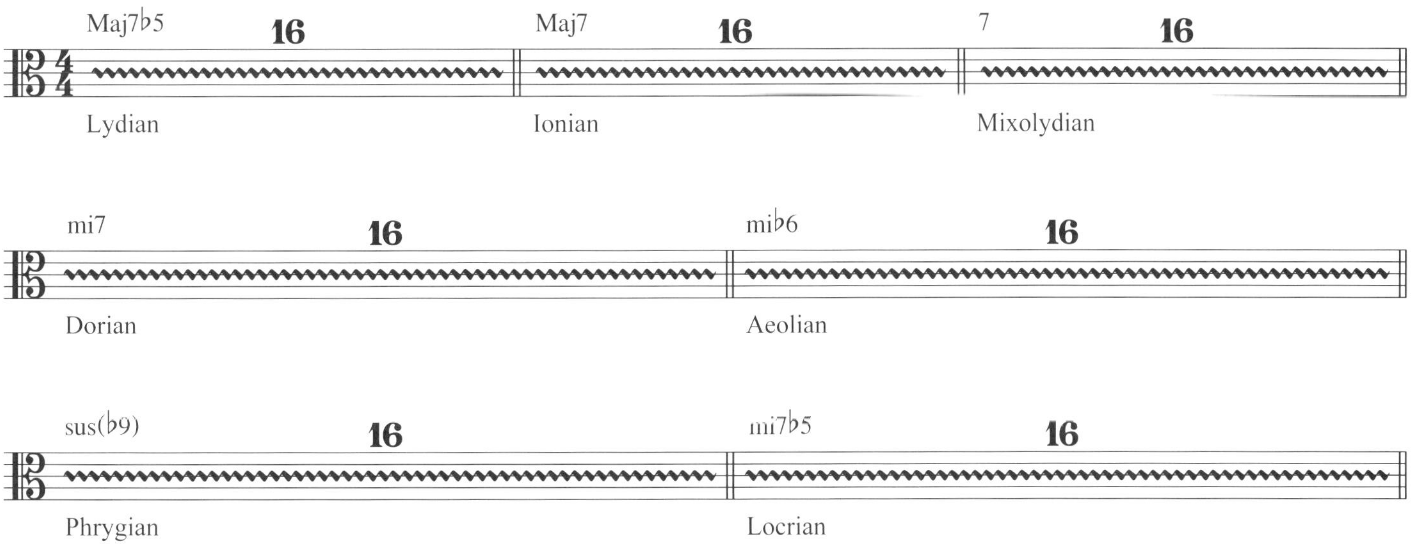

FIG. 7.3. Modes on a Tonal Center Chord Progression

ADJUSTING THE EXERCISES TO MATCH THE PHRASES IN THE ACCOMPANIMENT

You can also play the exercises with the play-alongs, but it's a good idea to make the following adjustment to the arpeggios that are grouped in threes. Play them in half time—in other words, quarter-note triplets instead of the three groups of eighth notes (in 9/8 time). This lines up nicely with the accompaniment.

Try this (below) with the "modes in a key" play-along in the key of F.

FIG. 7.4. Modes in a Key in F

Add a bar of rest at the end of the arpeggios that are grouped in fours (you could also improvise briefly in bars with held notes or rests). Now we have a sixteen-bar routine that exactly fits the play-along.

When you are comfortable with the routine, try omitting the repeats and improvising on the second eight measures of each sixteen bars. Speaking of improvisation, in the pages that follow, you will find some ideas to help get you started, if you are new to improvising over chords and chord progressions.

CHAPTER 8

Scale Patterns

You'll be happy to learn that your classical training has prepared you for improvisation.

Jazz musicians use scales and arpeggios as a framework for improvisation. We practice the scales in patterns that will likely be familiar to you. Here are a few examples to get you started. These patterns come from the C major scale. Apply them to all the scales.

You will see a variety of suggested bowings. Observe them or dismiss them for now. Some of them imply a swing feel, but are also good for a straight eighth-note jazz feel. They are included mainly to help develop flexibility in your improvised bowing choices.

This first one is something you will definitely recognize: broken thirds.

FIG. 8.1. Broken Thirds

In this example, pairs of thirds (diatonic triads) ascend and descend stepwise.

FIG. 8.2. Pairs of Thirds (Diatonic Triads)

If we add another third to our triads, we have diatonic seventh chords.

FIG. 8.3. Diatonic Seventh Chords

Try reversing alternating note groups for an "up-down" effect.

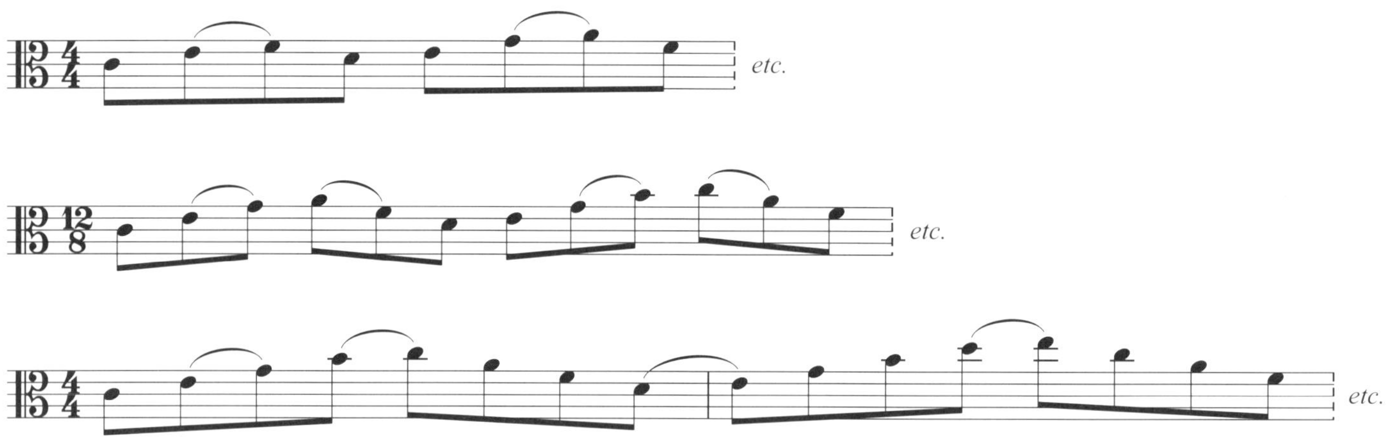

FIG. 8.4. "Up-Down" Effect

Here's another familiar concept: ascending and descending three- and four-note groups.

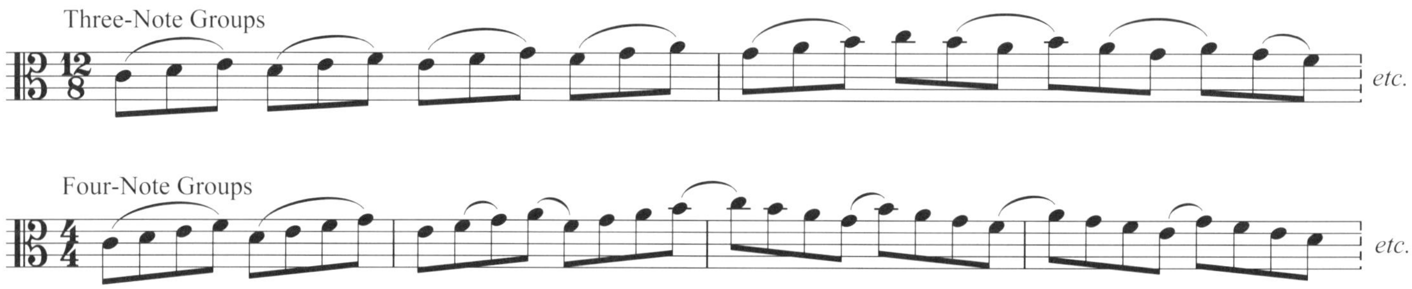

FIG. 8.5. Ascending and Descending Three- and Four-Note Groups

As you begin to improvise with the play-alongs, try incorporating these patterns. You'll soon see that, in some of the keys, the patterns present some fingering challenges. You may not use the same "pivot" moves you used when you ran the scale straight up and down. Awareness of the split and dual frames in the key signatures that require them will be helpful for navigation, as in this example in the key of A.

FIG. 8.6. Navigation Example in A

CHAPTER 9

Pentatonic Scales

Pentatonic scales are often used by jazz improvisers, both melodically and as five-note chords. Here's a C major pentatonic scale. It's 1-2-3-5-6 of the major scale.

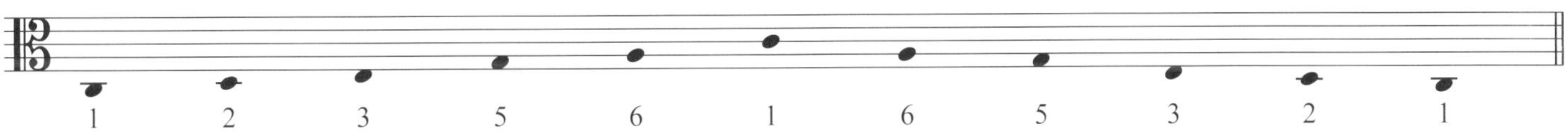

FIG. 9.1. C Major Pentatonic Scale

Now, we'll expand it to a four-string frame. Here's the diagram. You can also think of it as a C major frame with F's and B's omitted.

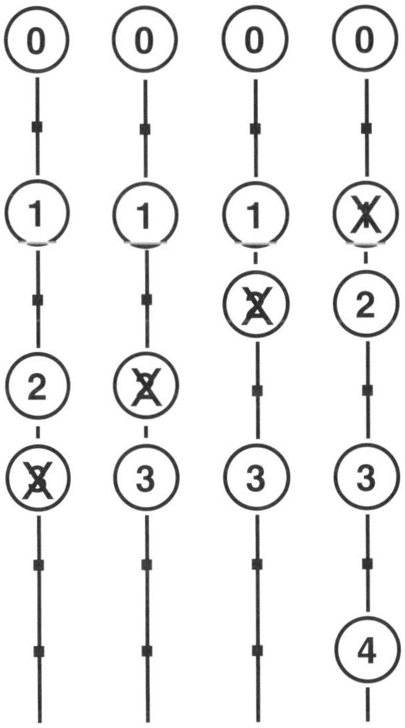

FIG. 9.2. C Major Pentatonic Four-String Frame Diagram

FIG. 9.3. C Major Pentatonic Scale Four-String Frame

By the way, this frame also contains the A minor pentatonic scale. C major pentatonic and A minor pentatonic share the same five notes. You can think of it as 1-3-4-5-7 of a minor scale.

FIG. 9.4. A Minor Pentatonic Scale

You can apply all the patterns you played on the seven-note scales to pentatonic scales. Here are a few examples:

FIG. 9.5. Pentatonic Scale Patterns

Try to improvise some bowings. Use the figures in chapter 8 as a guide.

Now let's take a look at some uses for the pentatonic scales over the seven chords in the progressions. We'll stick with the C "modes in a key" play-along. Play these pentatonic examples while listening to the chord vamps.

C major pentatonic sounds pretty good over the CMaj7 chord. That root in bar 2, beat 3, is a little bland, though.

FIG. 9.6. C Major Pentatonic Over a Vamp

Let's orient the scale away from C so that C isn't given so much "weight."

FIG. 9.7. C Major Pentatonic Oriented Away from C

That's better. Same scale, different notes emphasized. By the way, it doesn't matter what order the notes appear in, or how they are arranged. The preceding phrase comes out of C major pentatonic.

We can also use G major pentatonic.

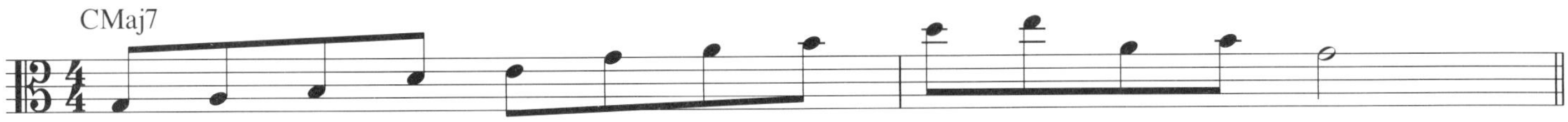

FIG. 9.8. G Major Pentatonic Example

We lose the C and gain a B. The 7 of the chord is more important melodically, and should be given more weight than the root. The bass player has that covered!

So, we can say that on any Maj7 chord, we can build a major pentatonic scale from the 1 or the 5. For instance, on a GMaj7 we could play either G major pentatonic or D major pentatonic.

On Dmi7, D minor pentatonic sounds good.

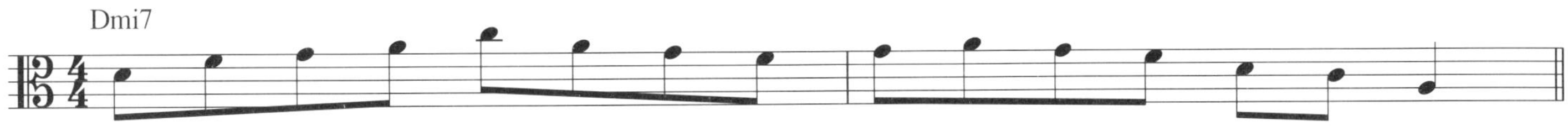

FIG. 9.9. D Minor Pentatonic on Dmi7

So does A minor pentatonic.

FIG. 9.10. A Minor Pentatonic on Dmi7

Minor pentatonic scales built on the root or the 5 of the chord will sound good on any mi7 chord.

Now we'll introduce some slight modifications to the pentatonic scales. By moving a pitch (or two) up or down, we get "altered pentatonic scales."

Take a look at this D major pentatonic scale.

FIG. 9.11. D Major Pentatonic

Now, lower the F♯ to F♮.

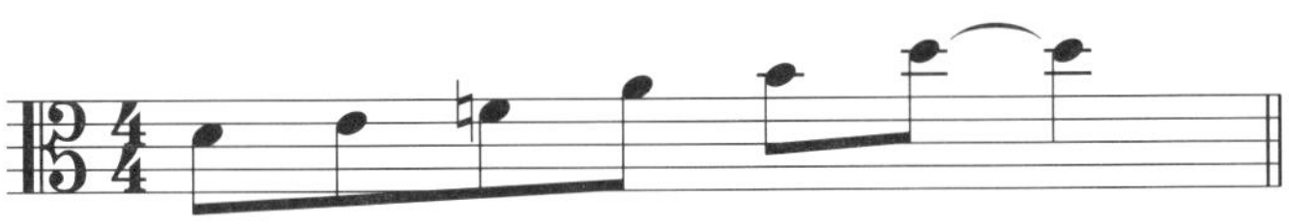

FIG. 9.12. D Major Pentatonic with F♮

This is called the Dorian pentatonic scale. It is made up of 1-2-3-5-6 of the Dorian mode. It will also sound good on Dmi7, among other chords.

FIG. 9.13. D Dorian Pentatonic Pattern

We now have our choice of three pentatonic scales that sound good on minor 7 chords: minor pentatonic on the root or the 5, and Dorian pentatonic on the root.

We'll use D Dorian pentatonic and a couple of others with the rest of the progression.

On sus(♭9) chords, we can build the Dorian pentatonic from the 7 of the chord. D Dorian pentatonic goes with Esus(♭9).

FIG. 9.14. D Dorian Pentatonic over Esus(♭9)

On Maj7♭5 chords, we can play major pentatonic on the 2 of the corresponding Lydian mode, or Dorian pentatonic on the 6. So here's G major pentatonic again.

FIG. 9.15. G Major Pentatonic over FMaj7♭5

And here is yet another use for D Dorian pentatonic.

FIG. 9.16. D Dorian Pentatonic over FMaj7♭5

On the dominant seventh chord, we have three choices: major pentatonic on 1 and Dorian pentatonic on 5, for starters.

FIG. 9.17. Dominant Seventh Chord

Here's another altered pentatonic scale. G minor pentatonic with a raised 3 becomes G Mixolydian pentatonic.

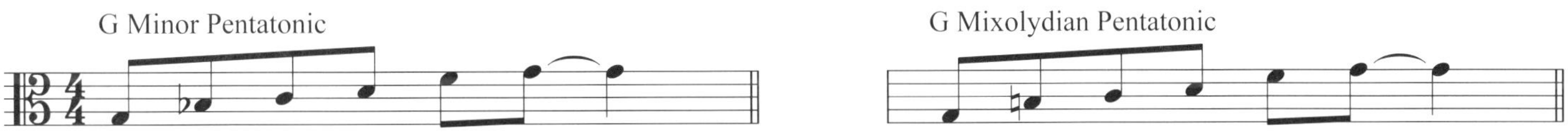

FIG. 9.18. G Minor and Mixolydian Pentatonic

G Mixolydian pentatonic is our third pentatonic possibility for G7. The scale sounds good with glisses!

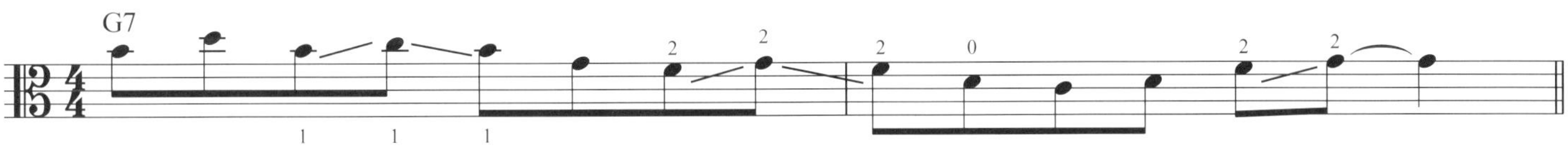

FIG. 9.19. G Mixolydian Pentatonic with Gliss

Here's one more altered pentatonic: Aeolian pentatonic. Lowering the F♯ in A Dorian pentatonic will produce A Aeolian pentatonic.

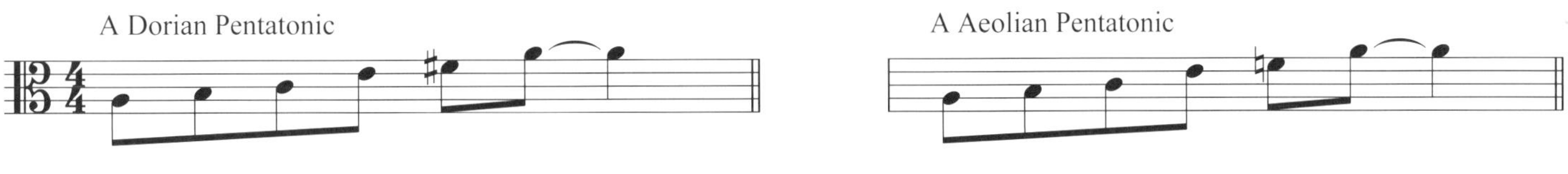

FIG. 9.20. A Dorian and Aeolian Pentatonic

This will line up nicely with the "Aeolian chord," Ami♭6.

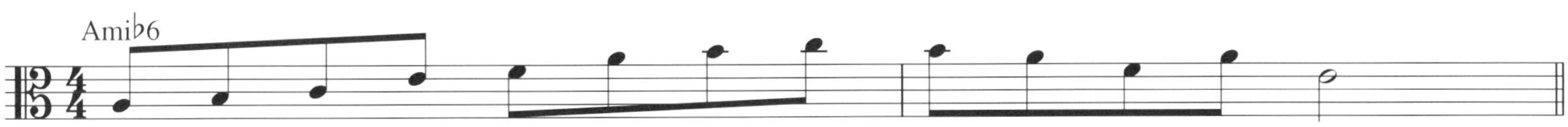

FIG. 9.21. A Aeolian Pentatonic

Dorian pentatonic can be built on the 3 of the Bmi7♭5 chord.

FIG. 9.22. D Dorian Pentatonic over Bmi7♭5

Let's review the pentatonic applications for the "Modes in a Key" chord progression:

Maj7	major pentatonic on 1 or 5
mi7	minor pentatonic on 1 or 5, or Dorian pentatonic on 1
sus(♭9)	Dorian pentatonic on 7 of Phrygian
Maj7♭5	major pentatonic on 2 of Lydian, or Dorian pentatonic on 6 (of Lydian)
7	major pentatonic or Mixolydian pentatonic on 1 of Mixolydian, or Dorian pentatonic on 5
mi♭6	Aeolian pentatonic on 1 of Aeolian
mi7♭5	Dorian pentatonic on 3 of Locrian

FIG. 9.23. Pentatonic Applications

If all of this seems a little confusing, just remember that we never left the C major scale! All of these ideas come out of the key signature of "no sharps, no flats." As you transpose the pentatonic scales to other keys, remember that all of them can be found by abbreviating the fingerings and frames of the modes that generate them. Try the pentatonics with the "Modes on a Tonal Center" exercises as well.

CHAPTER 10

Expanding the Roles of the Modal Arpeggios

As we know, there is some duplication among the arpeggios we've been working with. In figures 4.6 and 4.7, we saw that the chord generated by the E Phrygian mode shared all four of its notes with the next chord, the FMaj7♭5, generated by the F Lydian mode.

Ascending from E, these four notes form an Esus(♭9).

FIG. 10.1. Ascending from E, an Esus(♭9)

Ascending from F, these four notes form an FMaj7♭5.

FIG. 10.2. Ascending from F, an FMaj7♭5

You may have noticed that another pair of chord types, mi♭6 and Maj7, share intervallic structure (e.g., Amin♭6 and FMaj).

FIG. 10.3. Ami♭6 and FMaj7

You'll see that combinations of notes can have different functions, depending on various elements. In this context, it's useful to think of note combinations, such as our modal arpeggios, as "shapes."

In jazz, the word "voicing" refers to the way a player chooses and organizes the notes in a chord when comping (accompanying) on a chording instrument. Jazz players often use what are called "rootless voicings." The function of the bass in jazz is largely to play the roots of chords. In ensembles that don't include a bass, other instruments might cover the bass function: the cello in a string quartet, a guitar, a keyboardist's left hand, etc. As long as bass function is covered, the chord player doesn't have to play voicings that include the roots! If the root is not included, it may be replaced by a "tension," such as 9, 11, and 13. Tensions add color to chords. They are often notes from the associated scale.

When the 2 of a scale is used in a chord, it is generally called a 9. When the 6 of a scale is used in a dominant 7 chord, it is called the 13. We arrive at these numbers by continuing to stack thirds above the octave: 9, 11, and 13. We'll use 9 and 13 in the examples below.

The shape you know as CMaj7 played over A functions as a rootless Ami9. Chord tones 3-5-7 and tension 9 are present.

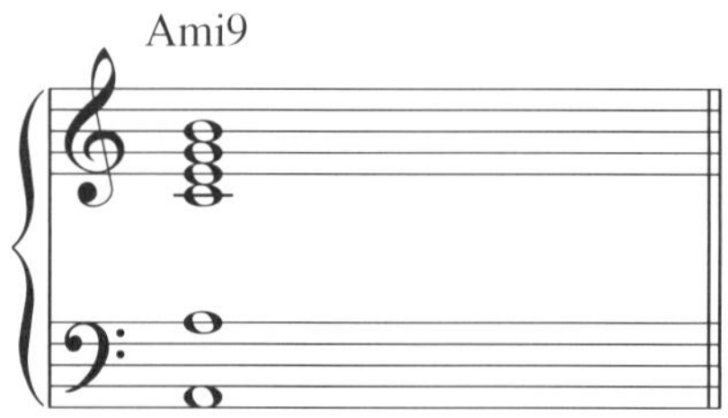

FIG. 10.4. Rootless Ami9. Note: When you see "9" by itself in a chord symbol, the presence of 7 is assumed. For instance, G9 and G7(9) mean the same thing.

The shape you know as Dmi7 played over B♭ functions as a rootless B♭Maj9. Chord tones 3-5-7 and tension 9 are present.

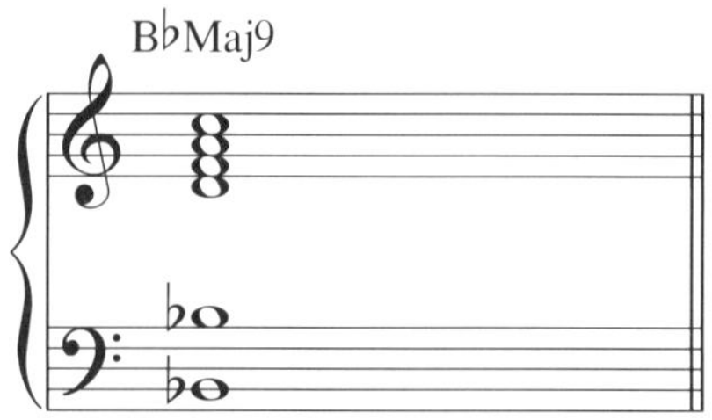

FIG. 10.5. Rootless B♭Maj9

The shape you know as Bmi7♭5 played over G functions as a rootless G9. Chord tones 3-5-7 and tension 9 are present.

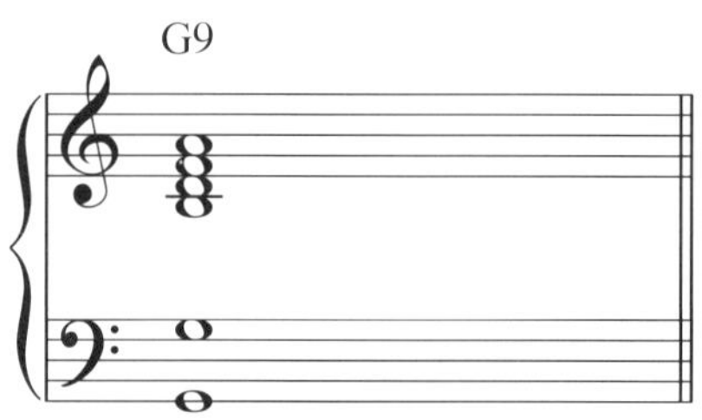

FIG. 10.6. Rootless G9

The shape you know as FMaj7♭5 played over G functions as a rootless G13. Chord tones 3 and 7, and tensions 9 and 13 are present.

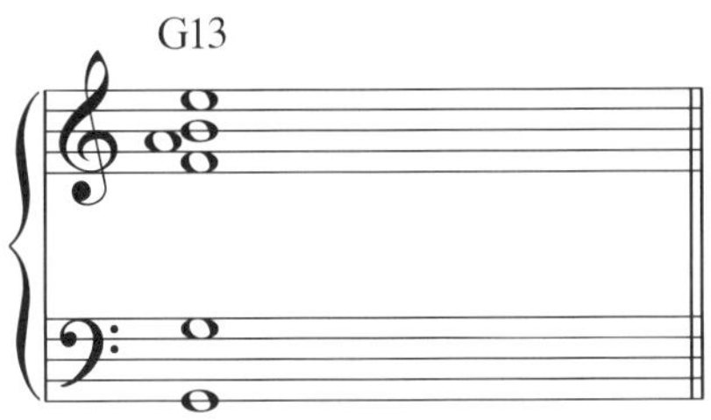

FIG. 10.7. Rootless G13

When reading chord symbols, it's common for jazz players to make spontaneous choices in using voicings like these. The 9 and 13 are often added, even when the written symbol offers less detail. The 9 and 13 (e.g., G9 and G13) voicings are appropriate in many cases when only "G7" is indicated. Again, the chord symbol with tensions may include or exclude the 7; in jazz, the 7 is assumed, if it is not part of the symbol.

Here's how to find the four rootless voicings in figure 10.4 to 10.7.

- On any mi7 chord, build a Maj7 shape on the 3. For instance B♭Maj7 over G is Gmi9.
- On any Maj7 chord, build a mi7 shape from the 3. For instance, Dmi7 over B♭ is B♭Maj9.
- On any 7 chord, build a mi7♭5 shape from the 3: F♯mi7♭5 over D is D9.
- For the 13, build a Maj7♭5 shape from the 7: F13 is E♭Maj7♭5 over F.

Chord Type	Chord Tone	Shape Built from Chord Tone	Example
mi9	3	Maj7	B♭Maj7/G = Gmi9
Maj9	3	mi7	Dmi7/B♭ = B♭Maj9
9	3	mi7♭5	F♯mi7♭5/D = D9
13	7	Maj7♭5	E♭Maj7♭5/F = F13

FIG. 10.8. Building Rootless Voicings

Learn to make these calculations quickly. Some work at the keyboard will be helpful.

These tensions sound great in melodies, too. Using the play-alongs, try to incorporate the shapes in your improvisation. Figure 10.9 has some ideas based on these voicings.

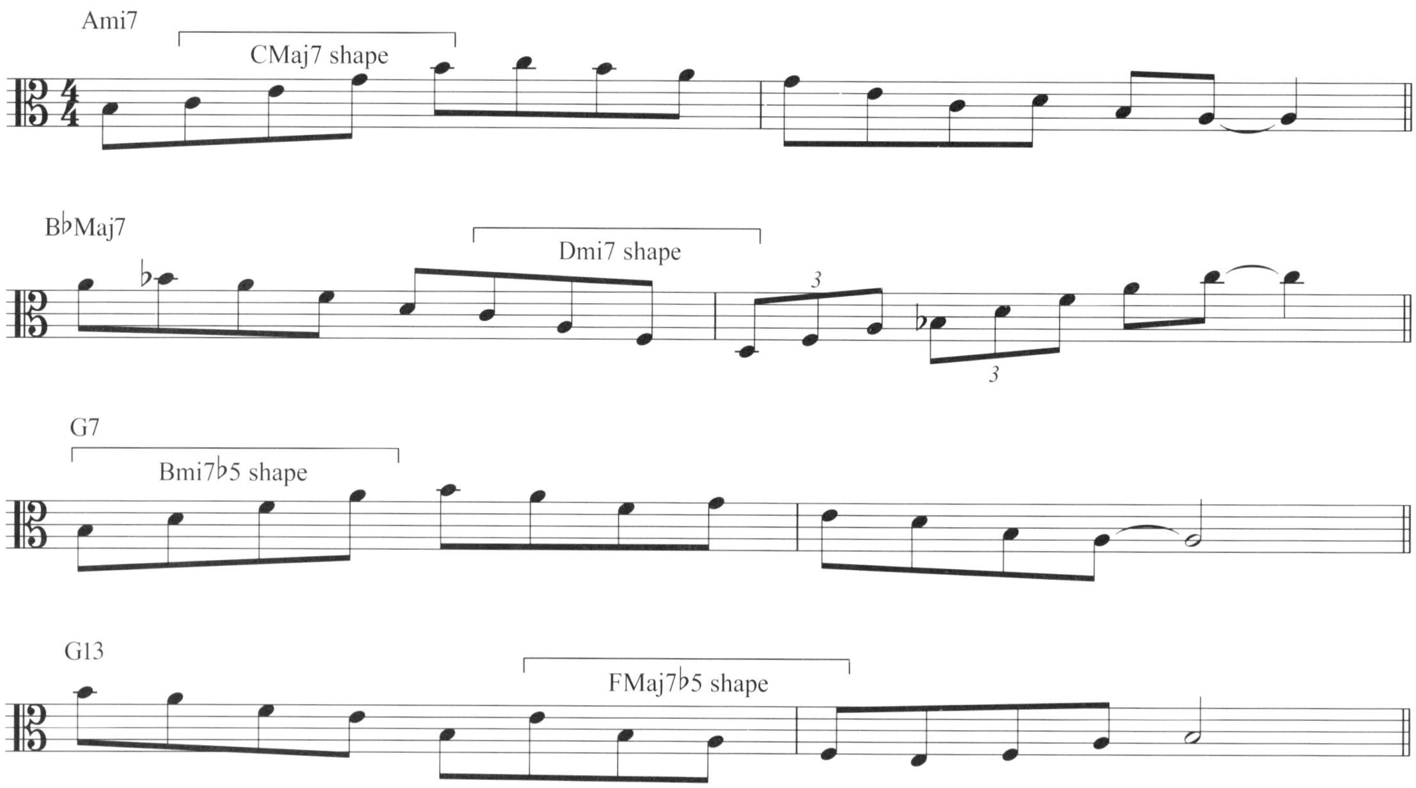

FIG. 10.9. Melodies Using Tensions

Remember, you will encounter plenty of Ami9, B♭Maj9, G9, and G13 chord symbols, but you don't need to wait until you see them to use these ideas. Let your ear be your guide. If it sounds good, it is good.

CHAPTER 11

Modal Etudes

The four etudes that follow are meant to be examples of what a jazz player might sound like improvising on the modal chord progressions, using only the associated chord scales. They should be played with the corresponding audio files, which play each chord for eight bars instead of sixteen. The suggested bowings are typical but are certainly not the only options. The fingerings should provide a guide to smooth transitions between the two neighboring positions when needed.

There are some specific concepts implemented in the etudes. Try to use them as you develop your own improvisations over the progressions.

1. Play the scales as fast slurred runs.
2. Play patterns—broken thirds, triads, three- and four-note groups, etc.
3. Create melodies using the arpeggios you practiced.
4. Use the various pentatonic options and patterns derived from those scales.
5. "Revoice" the chords using rootless shapes as a way to introduce more color.
6. Try to be creative with subdivisions and rhythms. Include syncopation.

Etude 1. G LIMDAPL

FIG. 11.1. Etude 1: G LIMDAPL

Etude 2. E♭ Major Modes

FIG. 11.2. Etude 2: E♭ Major Modes

Etude 3. D♭/C♯ LIMDAPL

FIG. 11.3. Etude 3: D♭/C♯ LIMDAPL

Etude 4. Modes of A Major

FIG. 11.4. Etude 4: Modes of A Major

AFTERWORD

As you practice improvisation, continue to practice the scale routines. Learn to play each scale quickly and accurately. Learn the patterns and collect some more through research and listening. Internalize the connection between scales and the chords/arpeggios they generate. Familiarize yourself with all the pentatonic scales. They are an important part of the modern jazz vocabulary. Learn those patterns too, and listen for more. Remember that anything a pianist or guitarist might play as a chord can also be a melody. The rootless voicings are a good start. Use the four arpeggios in figure 10.8 as you get better at reading chord symbols.

Particularly in the "Modes in a Key" progression, you should consider yourself improvising not so much in a scale or a key, but in a *key signature*. This mindset will prepare you to play over common chord progressions in which a series of chords may be addressed using the seven notes of a single key signature.

Listen for what we call "avoid notes," and handle them with care. Not every note in a chord scale can be emphasized over its associated chord. A good example is the 4 on a Maj7 chord. Play F over CMaj7 . . . not a pleasant sound. But if it's used in a run or a pattern, or in close proximity to E, it's no problem.

Again, let your ear be your guide. You may not always understand why something sounds good or bad, but you can tell the difference!

APPENDIX A

Frame Diagrams for Major Scales

Here are diagrams of all the major frames and their "relatives," as well as fingering alternatives. It is the "bird's-eye" view of the fingerboard representing all of the scales and fingerings practiced throughout this book. Learning to think about your fingerboard in this way will be extremely helpful in building improvisational vocabulary and harmonic understanding.

SIMPLE FRAMES

FRAME	RELATIVES	FRAME	RELATIVES
G Major 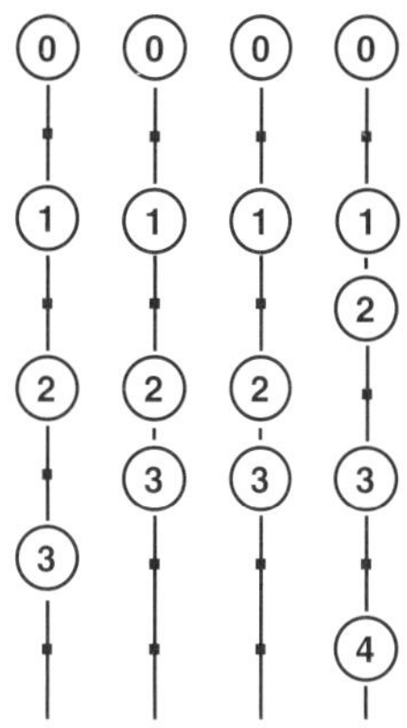	A Dorian B Phrygian C Lydian D Mixolydian E Aeolian G♭/F♯ Locrian	C Major 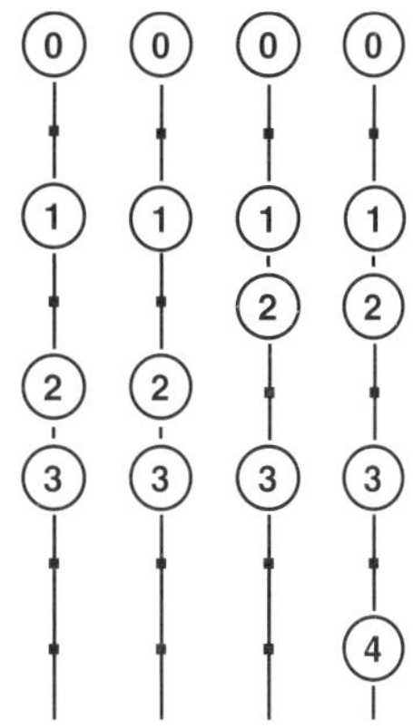	D Dorian E Phrygian F Lydian G Mixolydian A Aeolian B Locrian
F Major 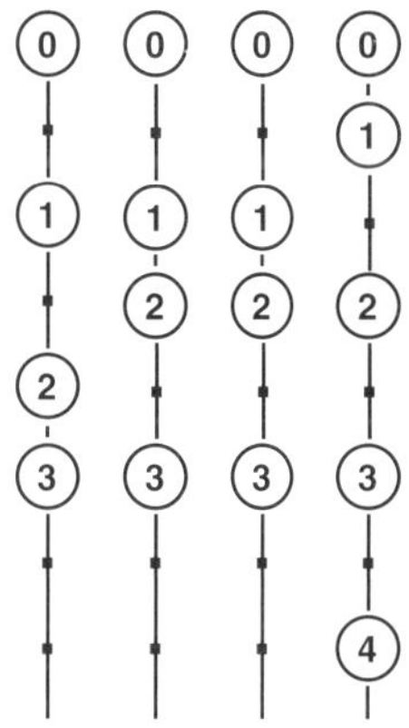	G Dorian A Phrygian B♭ Lydian C Mixolydian D Aeolian E Locrian	B♭ Major 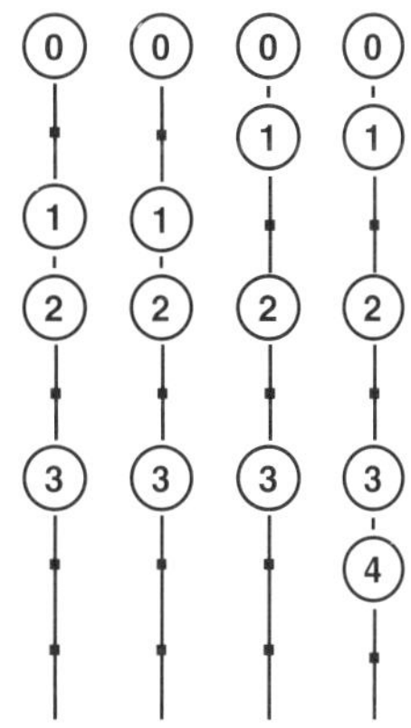	C Dorian D Phrygian E♭ Lydian F Mixolydian G Aeolian A Locrian
E♭ Major 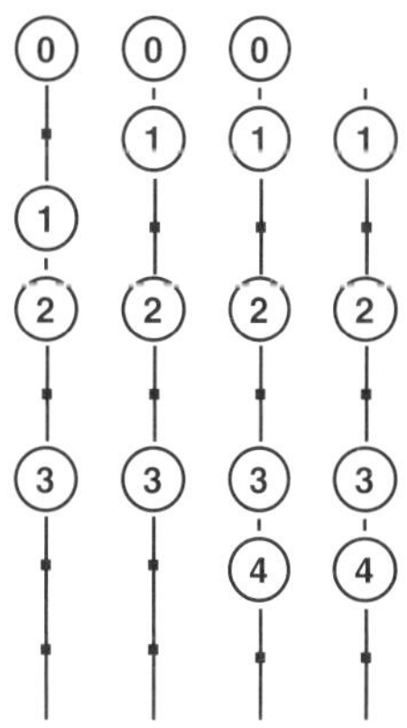	F Dorian G Phrygian A♭ Lydian B♭ Mixolydian C Aeolian D Locrian	A♭ Major 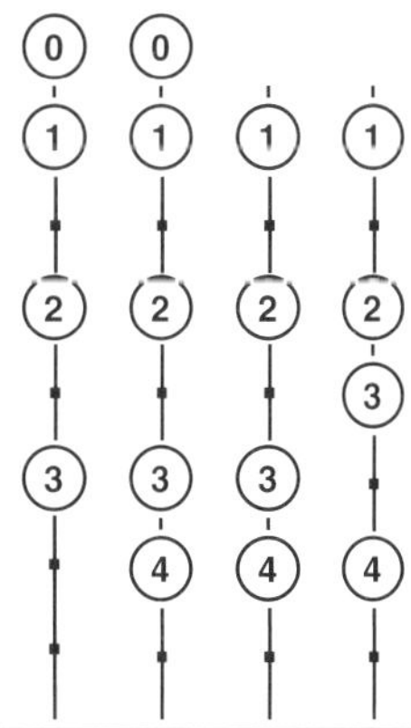	B♭ Dorian C Phrygian D♭ Lydian E♭ Mixolydian F Aeolian G Locrian
D♭ Major 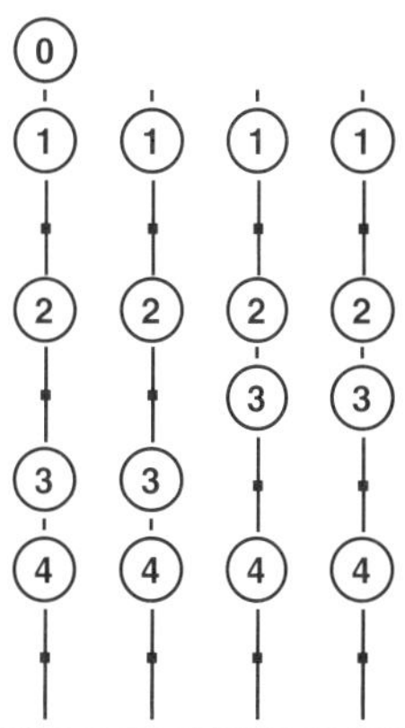	E♭ Dorian F Phrygian G♭ Lydian A♭ Mixolydian B♭ Aeolian C Locrian		

FIG. A.1. Simple Frames

SPLIT AND DUAL FRAMES

In the split frames that follow, only one shifting option is indicated. As you saw in the standard notation of the frames, there are other fingering options that you will not see in this format.

SPLIT FRAME	RELATIVES	LOW FRAME	HIGH FRAME
G♭/F♯ Major 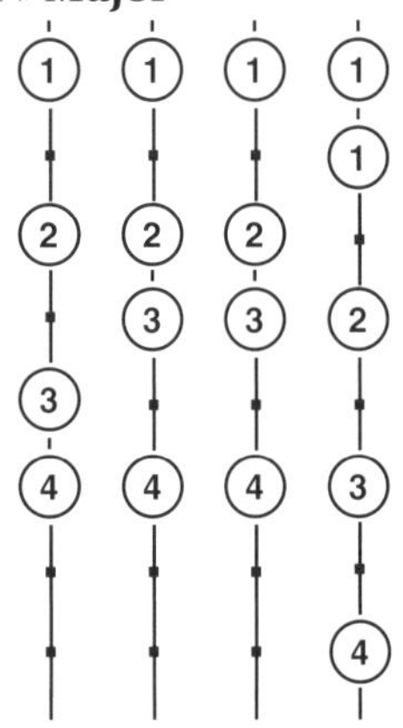	**A♭/G♯ Dorian** **B♭/A♯ Phrygian** **C♭/B Lydian** **D♭/C♯ Mixolydian** **E♭/D♯ Aeolian** **F/E♯ Locrian**	**G♭ Major** 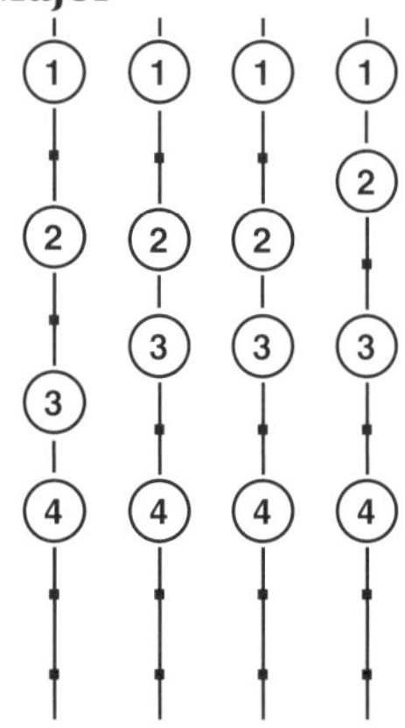	**F♯ Major** 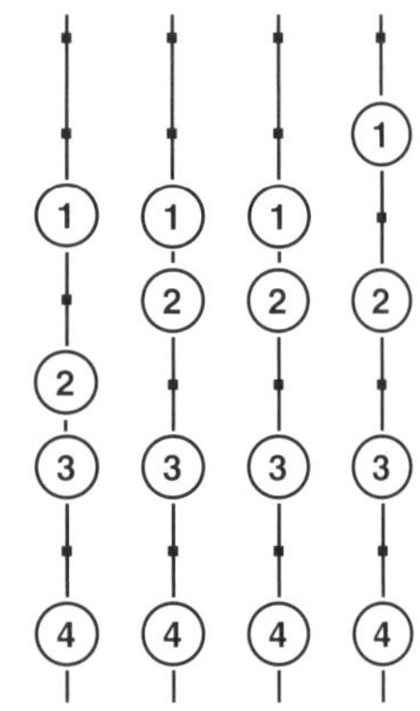
C♭/B Major 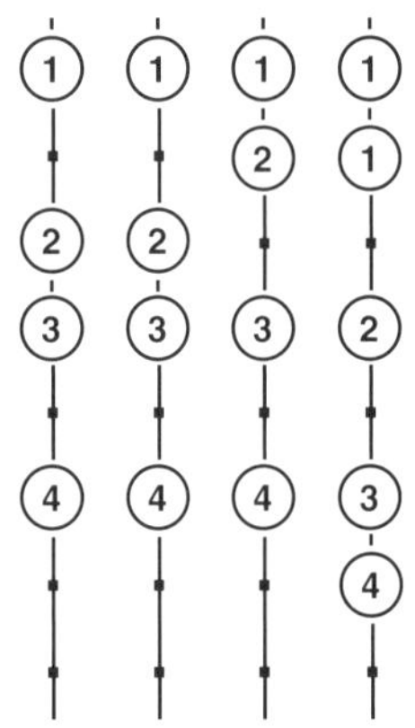	**D♭/C♯ Dorian** **E♭/D♯ Phrygian** **E Lydian** **G♭/F♯ Mixolydian** **A♭/G♯ Aeolian** **B♭/A♯ Locrian**	**C♭ Major** 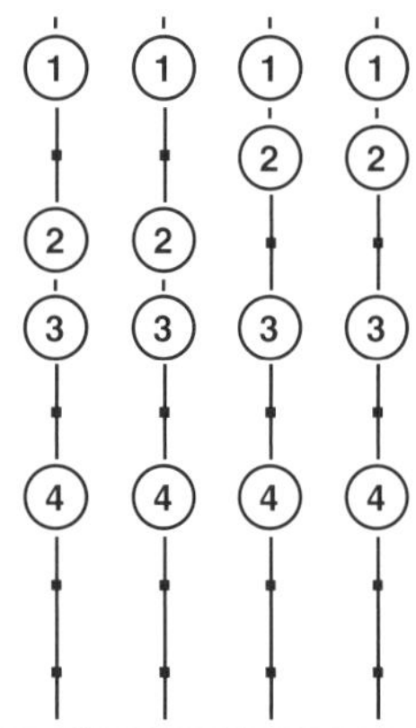	**B Major** 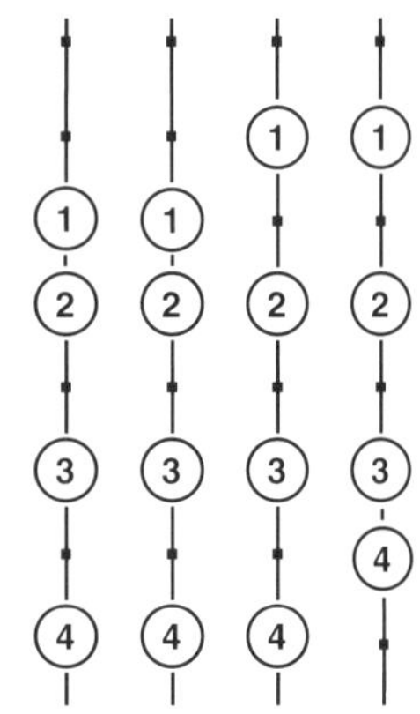

FIG. A.2. Split Frames and Movable Dual Frames

Any frame with no open strings is movable! Try moving these low and high frames up the neck, one position at a time. Double the root (twice) of whichever mode you choose. (See figures 3.1 and 3.2.)

SPLIT FRAME	RELATIVES	LOW FRAME	HIGH FRAME
E Major 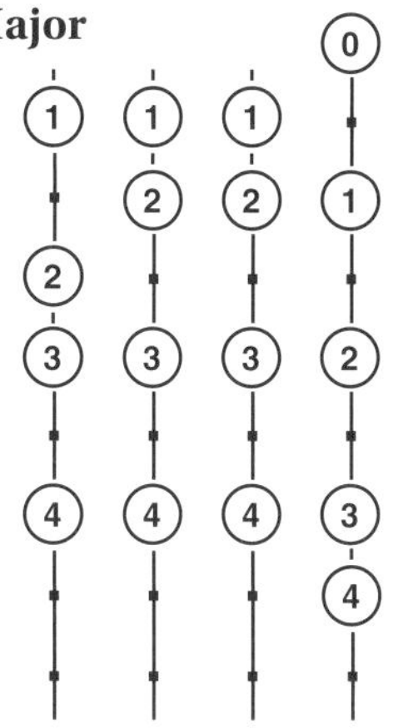	**F♯ Dorian** **G♯ Phrygian** **A Lydian** **B Mixolydian** **C♯ Aeolian** **D♯ Locrian**	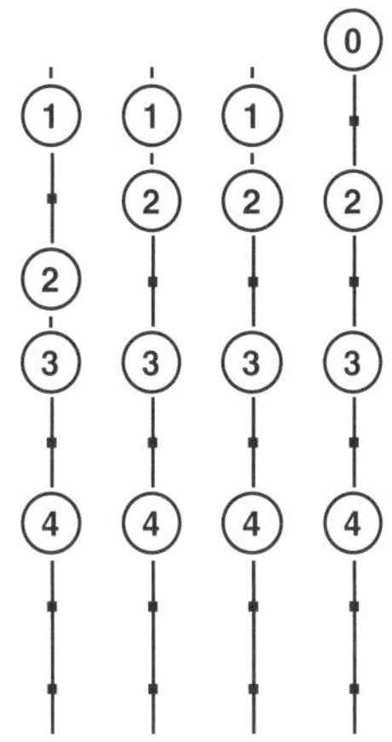	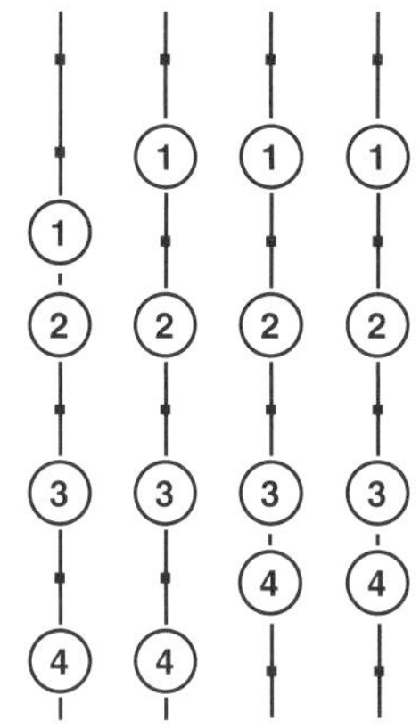
A Major 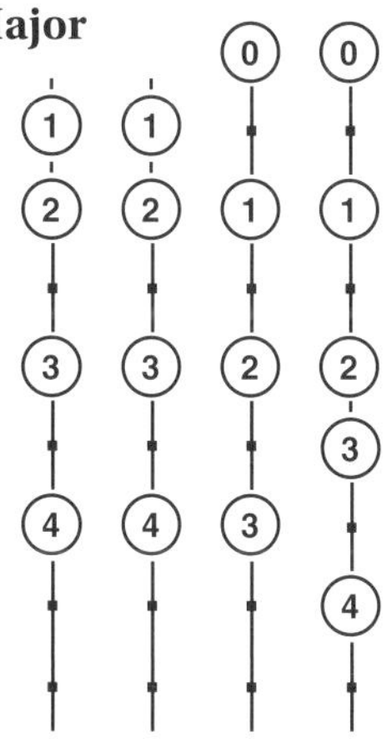	**B Dorian** **C♯ Phrygian** **D Lydian** **E Mixolydian** **F♯ Aeolian** **G♯ Locrian**	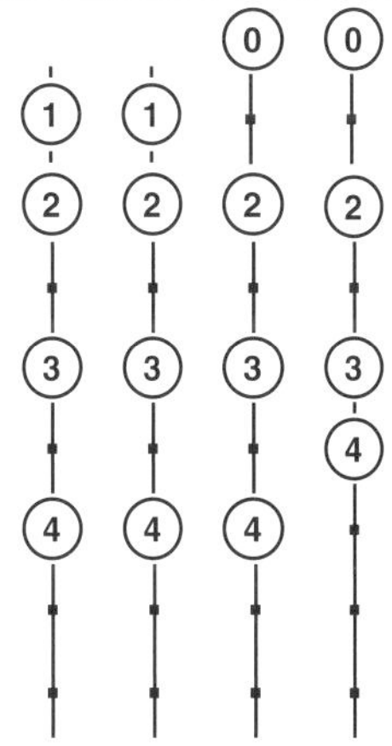	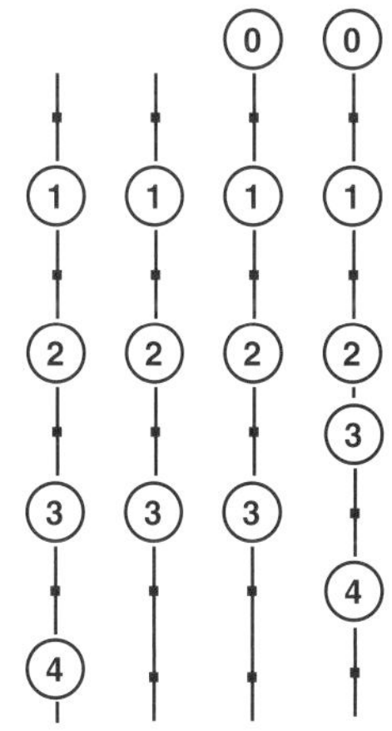
D Major 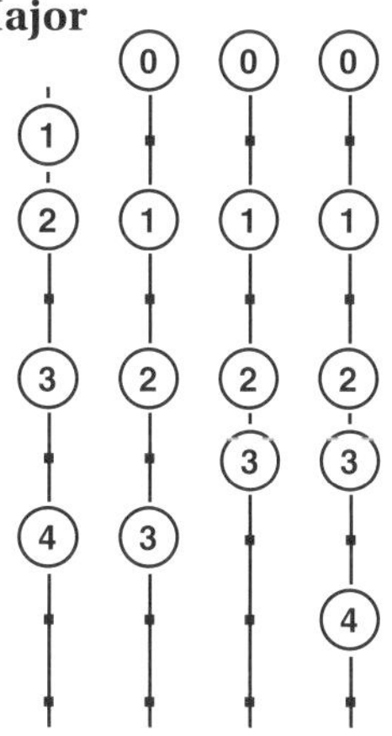	**E Dorian** **F♯ Phrygian** **G Lydian** **A Mixolydian** **B Aeolian** **C♯ Locrian**	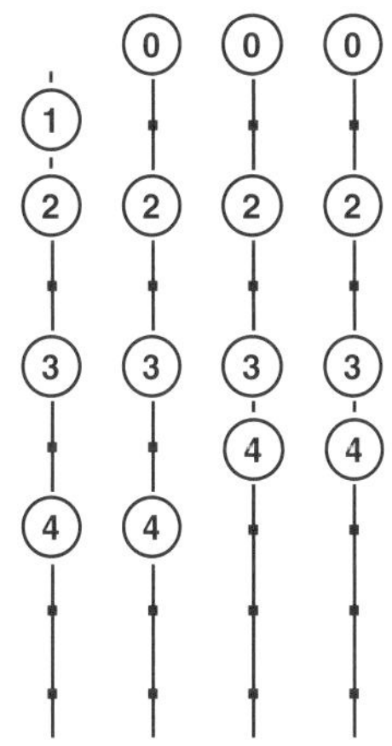	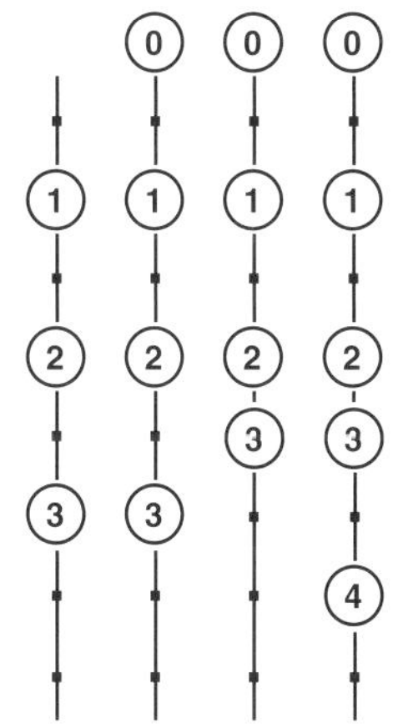

FIG. A.3. Split Frames and Dual Frames Containing Open Strings

APPENDIX B

Frame Practice Reference Tables

MODAL ARPEGGIOS IN THE TWELVE KEYS

It can be difficult, when playing the arpeggios from memory, to organize them in terms of meter and bowings. These pages will be very helpful. As you read each row from left to right, the numerals indicate the number of notes per bow (and by inference the time signature) as the seven arpeggios are played. Remember that the number of notes in one position accessible in these arpeggios is variable. A "3" means the arpeggio is played as two bars of eighth notes in 9/8 time (ten notes are available). A "4" means the arpeggio is played as two bars of eighth notes in 4/4 (only nine notes are available).

A "4/3" means the arpeggio is "expandable." In chapters 5 and 6, most of the arpeggios that came out of split-frame scales stayed in the low frame. In the expandable arpeggios, with a little extra effort, you can reach a tenth note using an alternate fingering that moves into the high frame. The expandable arpeggios appear in figure B.3.

THE "IDPLMAL" ORDER

I	D	P	L	M	A	L
Maj7	**mi7**	**sus(♭9)**	**Maj7♭5**	**7**	**mi♭6**	**mi7♭5**
C 3	D 3	E 4	F 4	G 4	A 3	B 4
D♭ 3	E♭ 3	F 4	G♭ 4	A♭ 3	B♭ 4	C 3
D 3	E 3	F♯ 4	G 4	A 3	B 4	D♭ 3
E♭ 3	F 3	G 3	A♭ 3	B♭ 4	C 3	D 3
E 4/3	F♯ 3	G♯ 3	A 3	B 4	C♯ 3	D♯ 3
F 3	G 4	A 3	B♭ 3	C 3	D 4	E 3
G♭/F♯ 4/3	A♭ 4	B♭ 4/3	B 4/3	D♭ 4/3	E♭ 4	F 4/3
G 4	A 3	B 3	C 3	D 3	E 3	F♯ 3
A♭ 3	B♭ 4	C 3	D♭ 3	E♭ 3	F 3	G 4
A 3	B 4	C♯ 3	D 3	E 3	F♯ 3	G♯ 4
B♭ 4	C 3	D 3	E♭ 3	F 3	G 3	A 3
C♭/B 4	D♭ 4/3	E♭ 4/3	E 4/3	G♭ 4/3	A♭ 4/3	B♭ 4/3

FIG. B.1. The "IDPLMAL" Order

THE "LIMDAPL" ORDER

	L	I	M	D	A	P	L
	Maj7♭5	**Maj7**	**7**	**mi7**	**mi♭6**	**sus(♭9)**	**mi7♭5**
C	3	3	3	3	3	3	3
D♭	3	3	4/3	4/3	3	3	3
D	3	3	3	3	4	3	3
E♭	3	3	3	3	4	4/3	3
E	4/3	4/3	3	3	3	4	3
F	4	3	3	3	3	4	4/3
G♭/F♯	4	4/3	4/3	3	3	4	3
G	4	4	4	4	3	3	4
A♭	3	3	3	4	4/3	3	4
A	3	3	3	3	3	3	3
B♭	3	4	4	4	4	4/3	4/3
C♭/B	4/3	4	4	4	4	3	4

FIG. B.2. The "LIMDAPL" Order

EXPANDABLE ARPEGGIOS

The extra note is always the top note of the corresponding high-frame scale, played with the fourth finger on the A string.

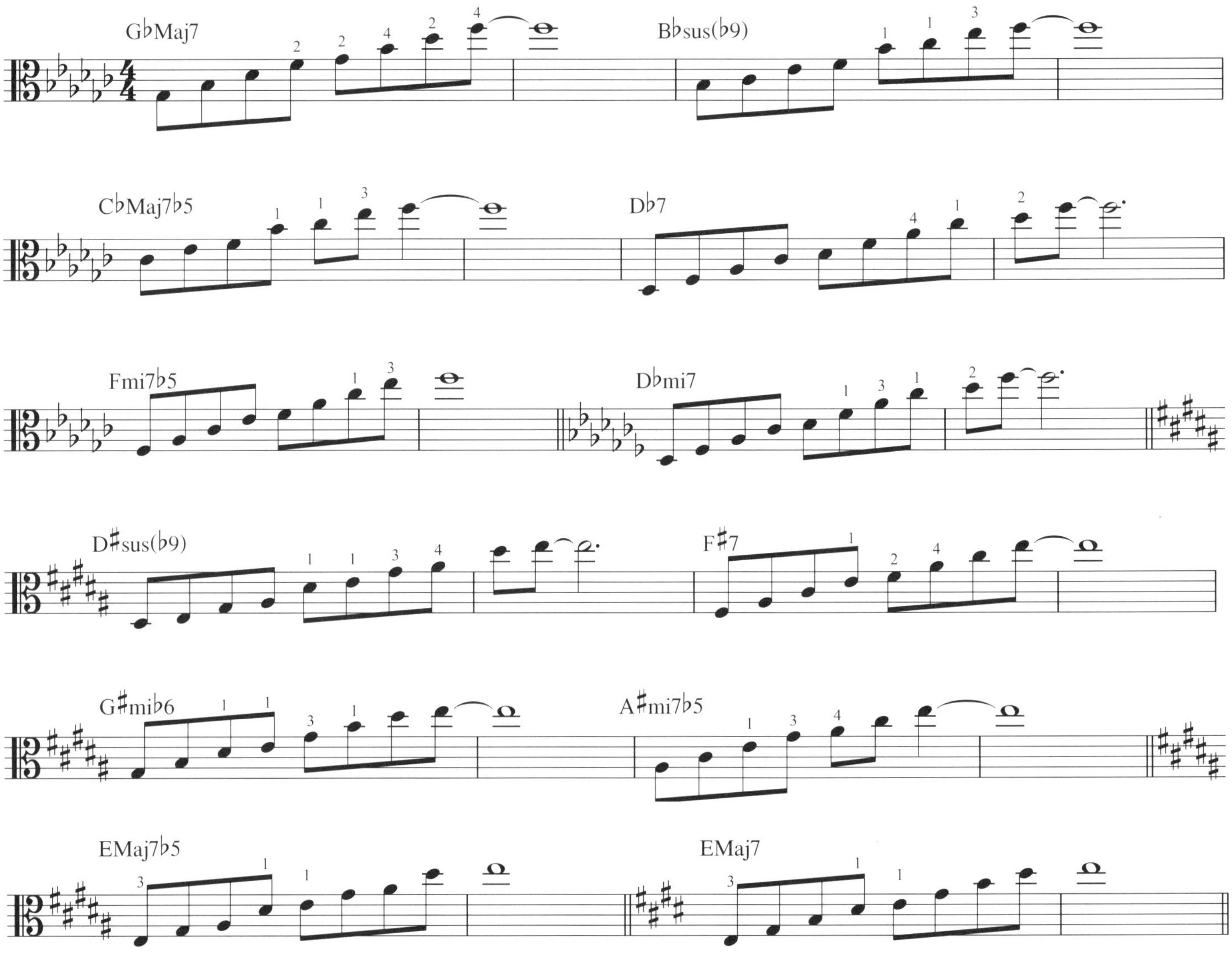

FIG. B.3. Expandable Arpeggios

ORDER OF "MODES IN A KEY"

Once you are familiar with the exercises, try playing them from memory with the help of this "cheat sheet." Start the modes on the major scale degrees listed in the far left column.

Major Scale Degree	Mode/Chord	Arpeggio Spelling	Pentatonic Scale Options for Improvisation
1	Ionian/Maj7	1-3-5-7	Major Pentatonic on Root or 5
2	Dorian/mi7	1-3-5-7	Minor Pentatonic on Root or 5 Dorian Pentatonic on Root
3	Phrygian/sus(♭9)	1-2-4-5	Dorian Pentatonic on 7
4	Lydian/Maj7♭5	1-3-4-7	Major Pentatonic on 2 Dorian Pentatonic on 6
5	Mixolydian/7	1-3-5-7	Major Pentatonic on Root Dorian Pentatonic on 5 Mixolydian Pentatonic on Root
6	Aeolian/mi♭6	1-3-5-6	Minor Pentatonic on Root Aeolian Pentatonic on Root
7	Locrian/mi7♭5	1-3-5-7	Dorian Pentatonic on 3

FIG. B.4. Order of "Modes in a Key"

WHAT'S WITH THE MAJ7♭5 CHORD? ISN'T IT SUPPOSED TO BE CALLED MAJ7(♯11)?

This chord is easier to describe in that way to someone who's never heard of either one and might not understand the convention that the ♯11 replaces the 5. Either way is correct.

DEFINITIONS

- Major pentatonic is 1-2-3-5-6 of the major scale.
- Minor pentatonic is 1-3-4-5-7 of the minor scale.
  (It's the relative minor of major pentatonic.)
- Dorian pentatonic is 1-2-3-5-6 of the Dorian mode.
- Mixolydian pentatonic is 1-3-4-5-7 of the Mixolydian mode.
- Aeolian pentatonic is 1-2-3-5-6 of the Aeolian mode.

ORDER OF "MODES ON A PITCH"

This is the LIMDAPL mode order. Once you are familiar with the exercises and have memorized the intervallic construction of the modes, try playing them from memory from a fixed starting note with the help of this table.

Mode/Chord	Arpeggio Spelling	Pentatonic Scale Options for Improvisation
Lydian/Maj7♭5	1-3-4-7	Major Pentatonic on 2 Dorian Pentatonic on 6
Ionian/Maj7	1-3-5-7	Major Pentatonic on Root or 5
Mixolydian/7	1-3-5-7	Major Pentatonic on Root Dorian Pentatonic on 5 Mixolydian Pentatonic on Root
Dorian/mi7	1-3-5-7	Minor Pentatonic on Root or 5 Dorian Pentatonic on Root
Aeolian/mi♭6	1-3-5-6	Minor Pentatonic on Root Aeolian Pentatonic on Root
Phrygian/sus(♭9)	1-2-4-5	Dorian Pentatonic on 7
Locrian/mi7♭5	1-3-5-7	Dorian Pentatonic on 3

FIG. B.5. Order of "Modes on a Pitch"

LIMDAPL EXERCISE FRAMES FOR C

This series of frames supports the LIMDAPL exercise on C in chapter 6. The arpeggios are grayed out. Go to the MyLibrary site for a complete set of similar frames for all the LIMDAPL exercises. See the first page of this book for the URL and your unique access code.

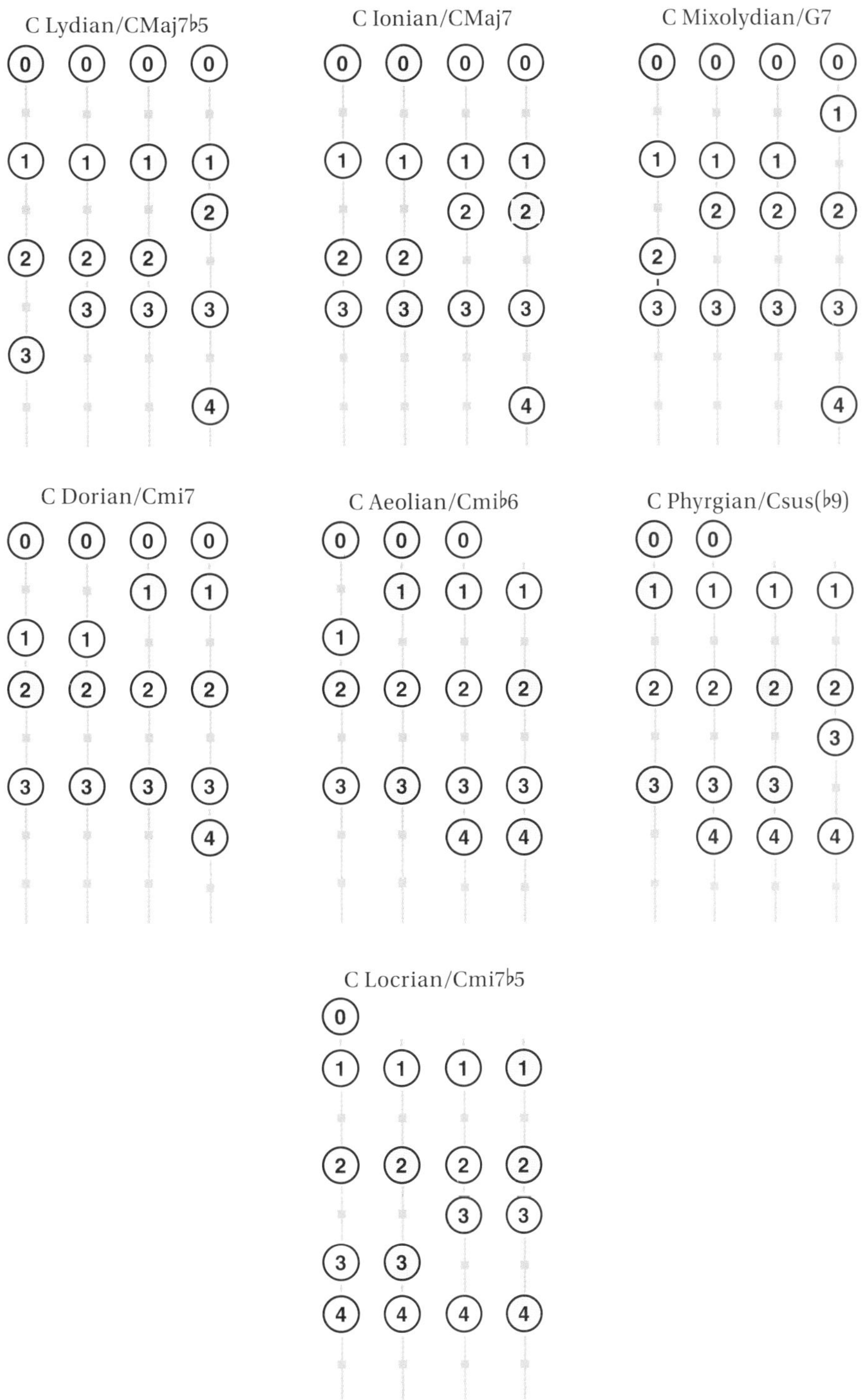

FIG. B.6. C LIMDAPL Exercise Frames

APPENDIX C

Symmetrical Scales and Arpeggios

The scales presented below represent a departure from the principal subject of the book: diatonic modes, and the framework they provide for improvisation. These non-diatonic scales are included simply to provide an example of the application of what we might call the "notate/diagram/visualize" system as it can be applied to other scales.

It's a good idea to visualize and practice every scale you learn as a four-string frame. This appendix shows the whole tone and diminished scales notated and diagrammed as four-string frames.

These are *symmetrical scales*. Symmetrical scales have repeating intervallic construction, such as "ww" (whole-whole), and "wh" and "hw," for the two modes of the diminished scale: whole-half and half-whole. They are also known as "scales of limited transposition."

WHOLE-TONE SCALES

You only have to learn two frames to play all twelve whole-tone scales.

Lowest Tonic	Shared by These Tonics
C	D, E, G♭/F♯, A♭, B♭
D♭	E♭, F, G, A, B

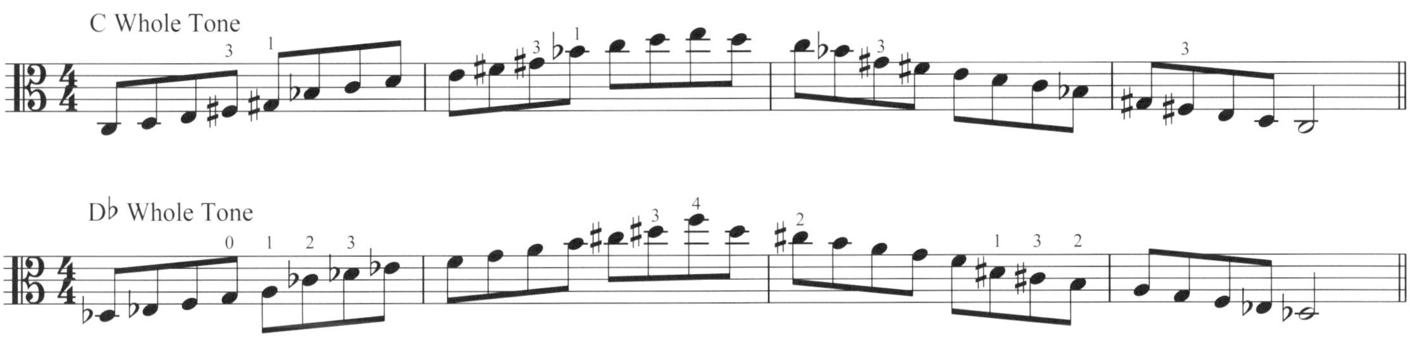

FIG. C.1. C and D♭ Whole-Tone Scales

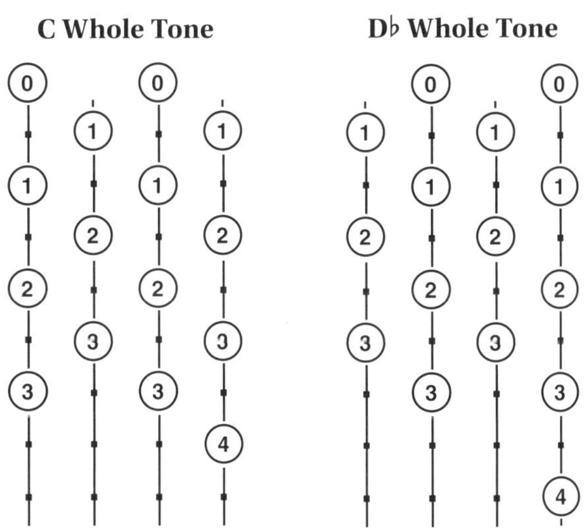

FIG. C.2. Whole-Tone Scale Frames

DIMINISHED SCALES

Both modes (whole/half and half/whole) of all twelve diminished scales are contained in three frames.

Lowest Tonic	Whole/Half Scales	Half/Whole Scales
C Whole/Half	E♭, G♭, A	D, F, A♭, B
C Half/Whole	D♭, E, G, B♭	E♭, G♭/F♯, A
D♭ Half/Whole	F, A♭, B	E, G, B♭

FIG. C.3. Diminished Scales

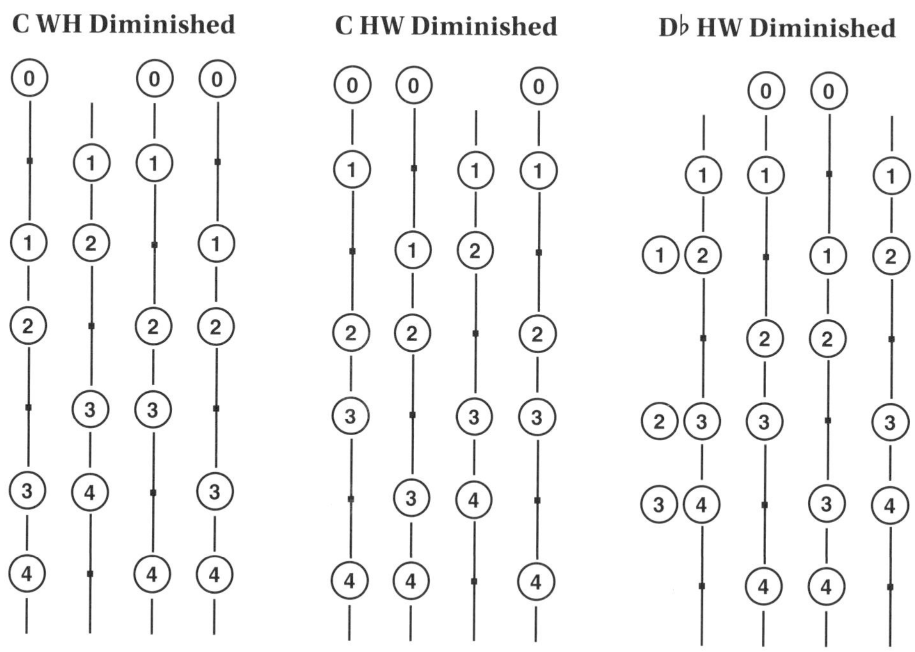

FIG. C.4. Diminished Scale Frames

ARPEGGIOS

The arpeggios associated with diminished and whole tone scales are diminished 7 (dim7 or °7) and augmented triads (aug or +). Because, like the scales, the arpeggios are symmetrical, the seven lines of notation below contain all twelve diminished 7 chords and all twelve augmented triads.

Diminished 7 Arpeggios

Augmented Triad Arpeggios

ABOUT THE AUTHOR

Photo by Rose Stockton

Rob Thomas is a jazz string multi-instrumentalist, an accomplished player of viola, violin, cello, and bass. *JazzTimes* calls him "a violinist of exceptional creative resources . . . riveting as a solo voice with a rich complex tone that can sing or shriek." Thomas has been singing and shrieking in and around New York City since moving there from Oregon in 1991. Since 2001, Thomas has held the violin chair in the String Trio of New York, being the fifth in a series of notable violinists to join guitarist James Emery and bassist John Lindberg in that enduring group, whose presence on the scene spans four decades. Three critically acclaimed recordings including Rob have been released by the Trio. He has also recorded and toured with the Jazz Passengers, Chuck Owen's "Jazz Surge" big band, and the Mahavishnu Project. He has worked locally with John Handy's "Monterey" Quintet, Max Roach, Jan Hammer, Claude Williams, and Ada Rovatti's "Green Factor." Rob records and performs regularly with pianist Chris Parker's quintet and Gypsy Jazz Caravan.

While studying classical violin and music theory in his hometown of Eugene at the University of Oregon, Thomas became fascinated with jazz and soon began working with local players. He later moved to Portland and eventually played throughout the Pacific Northwest as a leader on violin and a sideman on bass (on which he "doubled expertly," according to Leonard Feather in a *Los Angeles Times* festival review), gaining valuable experience in pick-up bands with jazz greats Joe Henderson, Bobby Hutcherson, Charlie Rouse, Eddie Harris, Mose Allison, Nat Adderley, and others. Rob's own groups made regular appearances at regional clubs and festivals and often included local luminaries Glen Moore, Nancy King, and Jerry Hahn.

An enthusiastic educator, Thomas taught in the Northwest at Reed College and Marylhurst University, and at Cornish College of the Arts. He is currently a professor at Berklee College of Music, where he has taught since 2002.

WOODWINDS & BRASS

TRUMPET SOUND EFFECTS
Craig Pederson & Ueli Dörig
00121626 Book/Online Audio............$14.99

SAXOPHONE SOUND EFFECTS
Ueli Dörig
50449628 Book/Online Audio...........$17.99

THE TECHNIQUE OF THE FLUTE
Joseph Viola
00214012 Book.......................................$19.99

STRINGS/ROOTS MUSIC

BERKLEE HARP
Felice Pomeranz
00144263 Book/Online Audio...........$24.99

BEYOND BLUEGRASS BANJO
Dave Hollander & Matt Glaser
50449610 Book/CD..............................$19.99

BEYOND BLUEGRASS MANDOLIN
John McGann & Matt Glaser
50449609 Book/CD..............................$19.99

BLUEGRASS FIDDLE & BEYOND
Matt Glaser
50449602 Book/CD..............................$19.99

CONTEMPORARY CELLO ETUDES
Mike Block
00159292 Book/Online Audio...........$24.99

EXPLORING CLASSICAL MANDOLIN
August Watters
00125040 Book/Online Media..........$24.99

THE IRISH CELLO BOOK
Liz Davis Maxfield
50449652 Book/Online Audio..........$27.99

JAZZ UKULELE
Abe Lagrimas, Jr.
00121624 Book/Online Audio............$24.99

MUSIC THEORY & EAR TRAINING

BEGINNING EAR TRAINING
Gilson Schachnik
50449548 Book/Online Audio...........$17.99

BERKLEE CONTEMPORARY MUSIC NOTATION
Jonathan Feist
00202547 Book.......................................$24.99

BERKLEE MUSIC THEORY
Paul Schmeling
50449615 Book 1/Online Audio........$27.99
50449616 Book 2/Online Audio.......$24.99

CONTEMPORARY COUNTERPOINT
Beth Denisch
00147050 Book/Online Audio..........$24.99

MUSIC NOTATION
Mark McGrain
50449399 Book......................................$27.99
Matthew Nicholl & Richard Grudzinski
50449540 Book......................................$24.99

REHARMONIZATION TECHNIQUES
Randy Felts
50449496 Book......................................$29.99

CONDUCTING

CONDUCTING MUSIC TODAY
Bruce Hangen
00237719 Book/Online Media...........$24.99

MUSIC PRODUCTION & ENGINEERING

AUDIO MASTERING
Jonathan Wyner
50449581 Book/CD..............................$34.99

AUDIO POST PRODUCTION
Mark Cross
50449627 Book......................................$27.99

CREATING COMMERCIAL MUSIC
Peter Bell
00278535 Book/Online Media...........$19.99

HIP-HOP PRODUCTION
Prince Charles Alexander
50449582 Book/Online Audio..........$24.99

THE SINGER-SONGWRITER'S GUIDE TO RECORDING IN THE HOME STUDIO
Shane Adams
00148211 Book......................................$19.99

UNDERSTANDING AUDIO
Daniel M. Thompson
00148197 Book......................................$44.99

MUSIC BUSINESS

CROWDFUNDING FOR MUSICIANS
Laser Malena-Webber
00285092 Book......................................$17.99

ENGAGING THE CONCERT AUDIENCE
David Wallace
00244532 Book/Online Media...........$16.99

HOW TO GET A JOB IN THE MUSIC INDUSTRY
Keith Hatschek with Breanne Beseda
00130699 Book......................................$27.99

MAKING MUSIC MAKE MONEY
Eric Beall
00355740 Book......................................$29.99

MUSIC INDUSTRY FORMS
Jonathan Feist
00121814 Book......................................$17.99

MUSIC LAW IN THE DIGITAL AGE
Allen Bargfrede
00366048 Book......................................$24.99

MUSIC MARKETING
Mike King
50449588 Book......................................$24.99

PROJECT MANAGEMENT FOR MUSICIANS
Jonathan Feist
50449659 Book......................................$39.99

THE SELF-PROMOTING MUSICIAN
Peter Spellman
00119607 Book......................................$29.99

ARRANGING & IMPROVISATION

ARRANGING FOR HORNS
Jerry Gates
00121625 Book/Online Audio............$24.99

BERKLEE BOOK OF JAZZ HARMONY
Joe Mulholland & Tom Hojnacki
00113755 Book/Online Audio............$29.99

MODERN JAZZ VOICINGS
Ted Pease & Ken Pullig
50449485 Book/Online Audio..........$27.99

Prices subject to change without notice. Visit your local music dealer or bookstore, or go to **www.berkleepress.com**

SONGWRITING/COMPOSING

BEGINNING SONGWRITING
Andrea Stolpe with Jan Stolpe
00138503 Book/Online Audio...........$22.99

COMPLETE GUIDE TO FILM SCORING
Richard Davis
50449607 Book......................................$34.99

THE CRAFT OF SONGWRITING
Scarlet Keys
00159283 Book/Online Audio...........$24.99

CREATIVE STRATEGIES IN FILM SCORING
Ben Newhouse
00242911 Book/Online Media............$27.99

JAZZ COMPOSITION
Ted Pease
50448000 Book/Online Audio $39.99

MELODY IN SONGWRITING
Jack Perricone
50449419 Book......................................$26.99

MUSIC COMPOSITION FOR FILM AND TELEVISION
Lalo Schifrin
50449604 Book......................................$39.99

POPULAR LYRIC WRITING
Andrea Stolpe
50449553 Book......................................$17.99

THE SONGWRITER'S WORKSHOP
Jimmy Kachulis
Harmony
50449519 Book/Online Audio $29.99
Melody
50449518 Book/Online Audio $24.99

SONGWRITING: ESSENTIAL GUIDE
Pat Pattison
Lyric Form and Structure
50481582 Book......................................$19.99
Rhyming
00124366 Book......................................$22.99

SONGWRITING IN PRACTICE
Mark Simos
00244545 Book......................................$16.99

SONGWRITING STRATEGIES
Mark Simos
50449621 Book......................................$27.99

SONGBOOKS

NEW STANDARDS
Terri Lyne Carrington
00369515 Book......................................$29.99

WELLNESS/AUTOBIOGRAPHY

LEARNING TO LISTEN: THE JAZZ JOURNEY OF GARY BURTON
Gary Burton
00117798 Book......................................$34.99

MANAGE YOUR STRESS AND PAIN THROUGH MUSIC
Dr. Suzanne B. Hanser & Dr. Susan E. Mandel
50449592 Book/Online Audio $34.99

MUSICIAN'S YOGA
Mia Olson
50449587 Book......................................$19.99

NEW MUSIC THERAPIST'S HANDBOOK
Dr. Suzanne B. Hanser
00279325 Book......................................$32.99

0323
309